Flourish

New Zealand Women and Their Extraordinary Gardens

JULIET NICHOLAS & BARB ROGERS

GODWIT

Contents

5	PREFACE	160	LYN BARNES // AUCKLAND
8	**LYNDA HALLINAN** // HUNUA	168	**JENNIFER HORNER** // SOUTH TARANAKI
22	**JANET BLAIR** // ARROWTOWN	178	**SAL GORDON** // AUCKLAND
36	**GILLIAN DEANE** // KAPITI COAST	190	**MARGARET BARKER** // DUNEDIN
44	**JOSIE MARTIN** // AKAROA	202	**ROSE THODEY** // AUCKLAND
56	**CAROLYN FERRABY** // MARLBOROUGH	212	**LIZ MORROW** // MATAKANA
68	**SALLY WOODHAM** // HAWKES BAY	222	**LYN EGLINTON** // WAIRARAPA
78	**KATH IRVINE** // OHAU	232	**PENNY ZINO** // NORTH CANTERBURY
88	**JO BEETHAM** // WAIRARAPA	242	**ROBYN KILTY** // CHRISTCHURCH
98	**LOENA McCORMACK** // AUCKLAND	252	**BEV McCONNELL** // WHITFORD
108	**JULIE RUSSELL** // HAWKES BAY	262	**PENNY WIGGINS** // WARKWORTH
120	**SARAH CAUGHLEY** // WELLINGTON	272	**ROSA DAVISON** // MARLBOROUGH
130	**RAYLENE WADDELL** // STEWART ISLAND	286	OPEN GARDEN DETAILS
140	**SALLY ALLISON** // NORTH CANTERBURY	287	ACKNOWLEDGEMENTS
150	**JILL SIMPSON** // BANKS PENINSULA	288	ABOUT THE AUTHORS

Preface

THIS IS A BOOK ABOUT green-fingered women. Juliet and I went looking for them up and down New Zealand and found them in abundance: insightful, knowledgeable and real, ready to tell their own stories. We were keen to record the extraordinary achievements of those who have elevated a home-based hobby to the level of art. From the beginning our reach was broad. Our final selection of these women signifies the hugely diverse nature of our gardening community, ranging in age from young saplings to venerable treasures; in motivation, from makers of pleasure gardens to practical growers of family supplies; and in the scale of their endeavour, from minute to massive. Some of these gardens are open to the public, most are not — so this may be the only chance you'll have to visit.

Sometimes living in forbidding microclimates and scattered from the north of the North Island south to Stewart Island, these women have a few things in common. Each one has responded to her own landscape and locale with energy and verve. And each has that generosity gene so often found in the horticultural world, the urge to share. Above all, these gifted gardeners are driven by a love of sowing beauty.

Beauty is in the eye of the beholder, so naturally you will prefer some gardens to others, but our hope is you will enjoy the road trip as much as we have. Between these covers you'll meet people who have become experts at gardening by dreaming and doing rather than hiring help in. Of course, most have had help — some more than others — from family, friends and partners, because only in the movies can you wave a magic wand and a new garden appears overnight. But these women are the driving forces, the list-makers, the diggers, the optimists, the dogged achievers who think in terms of decades rather than instant gratification.

Their approaches vary as much as their likes and dislikes. A lover of colourful sculptural succulents and bamboos may be unmoved by a backyard given over entirely to food cropping, with its utilitarian compost heaps and roaming hens. Someone whose heart skips a beat at the sight of rare native plants rescued from extinction may shudder at the thought of clipping shrubs into artful topiary shapes.

Mild-climate gardeners who can potter for most of the year may spare a sympathetic thought for their snowbelt sisters gardening where winters are long and often destructive. Flower aficionados will surely be glad they don't live in remote locations where access to garden suppliers (and the internet) is pricey or sporadic. You can be a purist and a collector but still sympathise with someone who relies on other people's generosity for random cuttings and shared seeds. Coastal gardeners who struggle with breaking waves, locomotive winds and poor soil have challenges in common with high-country dwellers for whom the gardening year is truly a four-seasons commitment. And whether you are a lover of antique roses, Victorian-era rockeries or gold-standard gardens of widespread acclaim, you'll understand that these women are gardeners just like us.

If you are a gardener, reading this book will, we hope, stir your curiosity. If you love gardens but not the act of gardening, we trust you will be suitably impressed. If you are a novice and intrigued but hesitant, take heart from writer Lynda Hallinan: she tells beginners to 'just plant something' and don't worry what anyone else thinks. Most gardeners who are honest admit that failure is not uncommon because nature always has the upper hand. But tomorrow is another day.

And it's timely that we celebrate how far women have come: the year 2018 marks 125 years since women won the vote in New Zealand. Looking through the prism of gardening, our book traces the arc of female achievement, which, though it takes place behind the garden wall, resonates in a wider world.

In this book you'll find reference to five-star gardens of national significance and six-star gardens of international significance: these are gardens that have been assessed by the New Zealand Gardens Trust as examples of excellence.

Some people have what are called covenanted native bush areas: this means a landowner and a local council or the QEII National Trust share a mutual interest in protecting a designated area.

On page 286 you will find the location and contact details of gardens that are open to the public.

Lynda Hallinan
HUNUA

LYNDA HALLINAN IS A FORCE OF NATURE and a force for nature. A self-taught gardener, she's a popular communicator whose effervescent yet plain-spoken approach helps demystify garden lore. Formerly editor of *NZ Gardener* magazine, nowadays she's a mother of two, living in the country, and still working full tilt — just not in the office.

Lynda's HQ is the kitchen table at her home on Foggydale Farm in Hunua, where Auckland borders the Waikato. This is where she writes her catchy columns for newspapers and magazines, and where she juggles regular radio and television appearances. She publishes her own books, too, and is a public speaker in demand.

Lynda grew up on a Waikato farm and caught the gardening bug young. She graduated as a radio reporter and worked in news, but away from the newsroom she always had a garden. So it was perhaps inevitable that she ditched current events for writing about her favourite hobby, and it was certainly a dream come true when she took over as the youngest-ever editor of *NZ Gardener*.

Since then Lynda's seen hundreds of other people's gardens and hesitates to nominate a favourite. She does recall, with clarity, visiting the late filmmaker Derek Jarman's modest gravel garden at Prospect Cottage in Dungeness, on the coast of Kent. Its driftwood sculptures, wildflowers and beachcombed beauty more than lived up to the expectations aroused when, as a 17-year-old bookworm, she read her first gardening book — *Derek Jarman's Garden*. 'It was the realisation of a dream. I was captivated. The idea of creating a garden from nothing when he was dying will stick with me till I die. It spoke to me more than Giverny, Monet's garden in France.'

Opposite: Former dressage arena now an experimental vege garden.
OVERLEAF
Top left: The converted stables painted black à la Prospect Cottage — a garden visit that had lasting impact.
Top right: Boardwalk area winding through trees underplanted with glossy ligularia.
Bottom left: Lynda is itching to tackle the paddocks beyond, perhaps with native trees.
Bottom right: A close-up of Lynda's picking garden, a working rather than a display area.

Sir Miles Warren's garden, Ohinetahi, on Banks Peninsula, was a different kind of revelation. 'I didn't come from a farm where you made fancy gardens. Here was a garden for pleasure. I was overwhelmed.' But as she's matured she's developed new respect for regular suburban gardeners — down-to-earth people who love their gardens and grow what they like.

As for her own garden at Foggydale Farm, it's unique: now you see it, tomorrow it will look different. 'It's an unusual garden in that I write about it month after month for *NZ Gardener* and *The Australian Women's Weekly*. That dictates that I'm always trying new things and changing things around. It's an experiment with far more annuals (including all the edible crops) than is possibly advisable.'

Some people marry into money; Lynda says she married into land — undulating, if

Clockwise from top left: A bright welcome at the farm gate; geraniums draw the eye to the boys' playhouse; Lynda's irreverent sense of humour at play here where chickens bed down in wine barrels.

you're being polite, or an uneconomic unit, if you're talking to an accountant. Her husband Jason Hinton already owned the 22ha block of farmland, so she was lucky to inherit the framework of a country garden. And even though she never aimed to have a big garden, somehow it grew like oxeye daisies. 'Wish I had planned it and made it smaller.'

Gardening keeps her sane, says Lynda. She'd far rather be doing it than writing about it because it's so much more satisfying, mentally and physically, to be outdoors pottering than inside typing. And it's more fun with a partner in horticultural crime; the work is too much for one person, she readily concedes. Luckily, Jason has impressive DIY skills, and she has an excellent friend/enabler/confidante/ inspiration in Fiona Henderson, an artist and gardener with decades of experience.

Lynda's garden style is driven by her relationship with plants. While she appreciates the theories of landscape architecture, it's not what she wants in her own garden: 'I like individual plants and their personalities.' And while her garden is more workhorse than show pony, she does gussy it up for visitors once or twice a year, to host a garden club or to raise money for charity. There's nothing like a deadline to motivate a burst of weeding and primping. 'My garden's a bit of a mess usually,' she says. Gardens don't have natural deadlines, she says, so she's happy to get cracking. Besides, she gets a kick out of people's feedback and enjoyment.

Gardening a stone's throw from the Hunua Ranges comes with its own set of challenges. Best feature: high rainfall. Worst feature: high rainfall, drought (when it's not raining), poor soil ('Hunua' apparently means barren soil), and frost. Philosophically opposed to

Top row from left: *Orlaya grandiflora*; *Acer palmatum* 'Red Emperor'; Japanese holly *Ilex crenata* grown as a soft hedge. **Middle row from left:** *Ligularia reniformis* whose leaves recall an artist's palette or tractor seat with the giant African lobelia *Lobelia aberdarica*; *Podophyllum* 'Kaleidoscope'; *Achillea chrysocoma* 'Grandiflora'. **Bottom row from left:** *Calycanthus x raulstonii* 'Hartlage Wine'; *Phylica pubescens*; honeywort *Cerinthe major* var. *purpurascens*.

using sprays or pesticides, she suffers the consequences of living with pests, weeds and diseases. It's a very costly philosophy, she ruefully concedes.

As for plant health, on this cold, wet hillside she's had her disasters. 'I lost all our chestnuts, which is kind of depressing but there's nothing you can do.' Perennials, her favourite flowering plants, fail to thrive. She loves the swagger of English gardens, but her attempt at a 30-metre-long herbaceous border was an expensive disaster, with everything bar 25 'Mary Rose' rose bushes and a few dahlias rotting out in the wet winter soil. She planted 500 echinacea and all but four succumbed — disappointing to say the least. She asks herself whether she's optimistic or delusional.

Undaunted, she's decided to extend the garden: colonising another paddock and making a hillside walk with sculpture under the kahikatea, a project that could spark a whole native forest next. But things rarely go to plan. 'My attempt to create a long border of wispy romantic purple tansy with its chubby caterpillaresque lavender flowers and ferny leaves was a total disaster. So instead I've just planted 46 'Limelight' hydrangeas under the avenue of *Pyrus calleryana* 'Aristocrat'. And we're repainting all the raised beds blue. And I have the hornbeams to clip, etc. It's a moveable feast.'

Gardening in this way takes a toll: years of weeding left her with such bad pain in her right wrist, it was disabling. She now swears by the Clark Cultivator, a nifty sharp-bladed ergonomic gadget invented by Barry Clark, 'a lovely chap in Canterbury'. One bag of Nitrophoska Blue lasts a year and sees everything right. And homemade mulch is the bomb: a fallen tree or shelterbelt in need of

Opposite: The always colourful entrance to Foggydale Farm.
Previous page: Despite the looming rain the picking garden looks pretty and inviting. A wire ball (wireart.co.nz) this side of the wrought iron gates leads you into the place where Lynda grows flowers for the vase.

trimming equals thousands fewer weeds. In future, she vows to do much more mulching and much less weeding, hopefully.

Maybe we take it all too seriously, she says. A garden should be a place of personal pleasure, and the place you feel most at home. 'I definitely think they are a creative outlet, but I'd say that nature is the true artist and we're all just fiddling about, moving things around and trying to win against weeds. Any garden, left to its own devices for even six months, undoes any human intervention and gets back to its own balance.'

Beginners say to her they don't know how to start gardening. She says, conquer your fear of failure and just plant something. Do your own thing. There are no rules. Grow from seed. Be kind to bees.

Janet Blair
ARROWTOWN

NEAR ARROWTOWN, WHERE SKIERS and wine-lovers rub shoulders with history buffs keen to learn more about the boom days of the goldrush, Janet Blair has been digging for her own treasure. And what's she got to show for it after 40 years? A priceless gem of a garden.

When she and architect husband John bought the 5.5ha of land in the early 1970s, its 1864 stone house was standing in splendid isolation surrounded by bare paddocks. There was no shade, no shelter or birdsong. In fact, says Janet, the silence was profound. 'One could hear a bee approaching from miles away.'

Nor was there any garden on the property, which had been a dairy farm for generations. The only trees were some ancient Lombardy poplars on the lower boundary and an equally old cotton poplar that sheds kapok in spring and summer, 'smothering everything beneath it and causing days of unwelcome housework and allergies'. Janet is allergic to a lot of things. She ruefully concedes that 'it's a bit tragic to become allergic to your own garden'. But what can you do?

The property has a clear view of The Remarkables — an outstandingly beautiful mountain range — to the south, and Coronet Peak to the northwest. Both are snow-clad in winter.

How to start a garden in such a vast landscape? From the beginning, Janet felt a powerful sense of place. For the first five years, while raising three children, she read voraciously, particularly English designer Russell Page's *The Education of a Gardener*. She was a gardening novice and his book was about excellence, setting standards she could relate to. She had always admired classic garden design, that mixture of the structural

Top: The delightful old stone cottage cried out for symmetrical planting, with a pair of Irish yews to represent the original settler brothers who farmed here, and a couple of 'Abraham Darby' roses flanking the front steps.
Bottom: Standing among Janet's topiary, looking down into the sheltered courtyard at the back of the house, where an ornamental grape supplies a flash of autumn colour.
Overleaf: This stunning mountain vista with The Remarkables (on the left) shows barely a glimpse of Janet's house and garden. The mountains are a constant inspiration.

with the romantic, masses of plants tumbling and spilling, long sweeps of hedges.

Her garden is the result of inspired vision — and relentless toil — that honours its natural surroundings. In its maturity, it's a gift of nature, a responsibility and a delight, she says. It's also a five-star garden of national significance. Janet says it all began with the mountains: their scale, permanence and drama were a huge influence. She set out to soften them by creating an oasis of serenity; and knowing it would require disciplined planting, she started with hedges of hornbeam, buxus and beech. And lots of trees: 'John and I share a great love of trees.'

Where dairy cows used to graze the wide, open paddocks, Janet wielded spade and garden hose to plant by hand chestnuts, claret ash, amelanchier, maples, liquidambars, *Parrotia persica,* liriodendron, London planes, elms, dogwoods, Japanese cherries (*Prunus serrulata,* aka the sakura), and a selection of viburnums, to name a few. Six of the oaks were grown from acorns — all are hardy, with the promise of autumn colour.

Despite best intentions, though, over the years dozens of trees have been lost to snow and wind. 'Rampaging winds from the southwest and north have resulted in carnage and much heartache, for these trees were all pivotal to the garden's design. No sacrificial trees were planted.' In October 2017 a spring snowfall had devastating consequences. 'I awoke about 2am to hear the sound of tearing wood, followed by muffled thumps. I knew what was happening.' Dawn revealed scenes of destruction: 32 trees and shrubs damaged, their limbs broken, rearranged, contorted. Janet thought she had lost the entire garden. 'I know it is often said that opportunities

Clockwise from top left: A moodboard of the Manchurian cherry, *Prunus maackii*. Bright and glowing in autumn; the many colours of its spent leaves; blossoming in early spring despite ground frost.
OVERLEAF
Top left: In the depths of winter, nature's architecture is revealed in the skeletal forms of trees and shrubs near the stone barn.
Bottom left: Spring blossom from two *Prunus serrulata* 'Tai Haku' carpets the lawn surrounded by the elegant curves of box hedging.
Top right: In summer the barn is almost swamped by a vigorous 'New Dawn' rose and mock orange *Philadelphus* 'Virginal', while spikes of blue delphinium tower over a hedge of culinary purple sage *Salvia officinalis*.
Bottom right: Standing at the back door framed with an eyebrow of ornamental grape foliage looking out into the sunny courtyard.

present themselves in a disaster. However, there is some grieving to be experienced before one can move on to that stage.' Recently a 19-year-old linden tree of great sentimental value was corkscrewed out of the ground by the unreal force of a northerly gale. What was all proportion and atmosphere and peace is desolation after such an episode, Janet says.

It's not all trees of course. Protecting views of the mountains and creating clear areas for gardening were equally paramount. 'Very early on I knew that the spaces one made were as important as those that were planted.'

The garden is wrapped around the house, and the areas close to it were designed from the inside, considering outlooks from every window. Janet loves being able to open a window and smell the fragrance of lavender, and see the way the sunlight glints on mown grass paths.

The continuous form of the mountains in the background inspired an instinctive urge for repeat planting, and their colours furnished an obvious palette. You can't have little bits of this and that in such company, so her planting style emulates their solid and immovable presence. The greys and blues throughout the garden, especially in the barn border, echo the changing hues of the mountains. In a nod to their scale, Janet has created a rhythmic pattern of mass-planted purple sage, glacial blue iris and misty blue nepeta. She celebrates detail and subtlety. 'I wanted to achieve a feeling of beauty, harmony and tranquillity.' Yes, it's very labour intensive, she agrees, but she has no plans to change.

Many of the plants were grown from cuttings and division, particularly the box hedging, topiary and rugosa roses. Near the back door a paved terrace was dug out from a raised

Clockwise from top: Two seasons, one view. In summer, at left, a hedge of the rugosa rose 'Alba' sets a joyful mood; In autumn, the turning leaves announce winter is coming; At the entrance to the vege garden, a playful mood is evoked with more of Janet's topiary.

bank, its edges lined with the same schist the house was built from. Above that she gradually added topiary shapes grown from cuttings. In fact, Janet dedicated a whole paddock to raising buxus seedlings from an initial handful of plants she bought. Hedges, classic cones, obelisks, roundels, a pack of cards . . . she revels in the possibilities of buxus.

Janet is moved by the natural evolution of the garden throughout the year. Just as in music, you have everything from the prelude — the first stirrings of spring — to the adagio or slowing down of growth in autumn 'which I always think of as nature's compensation for the harsh season to come, the coda'. Making a garden is like composing music, she says: we all have access to the same notes but it's the notes we choose and the way we use them that sets a composition or garden apart.

People say gardening is the most difficult art form. Unlike a painting or a building, a garden is never static; it's in a permanent state of transition, constantly growing, changing and evolving. Janet likes to quote an observation made by Sir Miles Warren, noted architect and creator of the much-admired garden Ohinetahi. Garden design, he told her, is fundamentally more difficult than architecture because a brick is fixed but plants grow. His words are a comfort.

OPPOSITE: Top row from left: The giant Himalayan lily, *Cardiocrinum giganteum* var. *yunnanense*; the striking red leaves of *Viburnum plicatum* 'Mariesii'; the scented snowdrop, *Galanthus* 'S. Arnott'. **Middle row from left:** The small linden tree, *Tilia cordata*; white berries *of Sorbus cashmiriana* and the red leaves of Virginia creeper frame the kitchen window; purple culinary sage. **Bottom row from left:** *Cornus kousa*, Japanese dogwood; these red tulips came from John's father's garden; the fragrant daffodil *Narcissus* 'Thalia'. **Above:** Janet takes planting and colour cues from her surroundings, as you can see here where rock wall and shades of purple look up to the towering Remarkables.

Gillian Deane
KAPITI COAST

SOMETIMES IT TAKES A lifetime to understand why you do the things you do. Gillian Deane always loved New Zealand flora and when her husband, Roderick, presented her with a block of coastal wetland for her fiftieth birthday in 1993, she vowed to restore it to a bush-clad beauty spot.

A few years later, family research unearthed a Māori great-great grandmother, Elizabeth Hill, of Ngāti Whanaunga descent, and Elizabeth's ancestor Puawha, who was a chief on Great Mercury Island, off the Coromandel Peninsula. Gillian was ecstatic. 'This is a whole wonderful story in its own right,' she says — and what's more, she realised her love of native plants was inherited: 'It's in my genes,' she says proudly.

Before she discovered her whakapapa, her instinct was to grow local, using plants that used to thrive here on the Kapiti Coast before the land was cleared for farming. She loved New Zealand native bush 'in all its forms and all its glory'. In Wellington, where they live some of the time, the Botanic Garden has always been an inspiration.

But faced with the daunting scale of the project — 7.2ha at first, increasing to 36ha as land became available — and the harsh wind-blasted maritime climate, over time Gillian has refined her vision for her garden, Te Maimai. Now she focuses on 'rooms' rather than the whole shebang. Her progress is deliberately incremental, and she names each area after people and events in her life. The soldiers' garden replaces two stands of mature and rickety pines that were planted around the duck-shooting pond during World War II; the fiftieth anniversary garden features yellow and gold foliage to celebrate the couple's golden wedding anniversary;

Top: A grove of ake ake (*Dodonaea viscosa*) whose gnarly trunks speak of years spent defying the harsh coastal climate.
Bottom: The old maimai (duck-shooters' hide) which inspired the garden's name.
Overleaf: The heart of this restored natural garden is its wetlands.

and the garden of morning mist and the millennium walkway are self-explanatory. At Christmas, red pōhutukawa planted by the main gate resemble stained-glass windows in a cathedral.

Gillian is a dreamer. A prolific blogger and penpal, she writes lyrically about her 'it's not really a garden' natural garden. Playing word games to describe her favourite natives, she has come up with (among others) kauri/strength; tōtara/courage; rengarenga/purity and putaputawētā/onomatopoeia.

She is an active gardener. Not one to sit idly by, she loves getting stuck in, with the help of local man Peter Paterson. 'I feel exquisite happiness sitting down and looking up through the kahikatea,' she says. 'Their lacey leaves are a contrast to their sturdy trunks. I love listening to the flax rustle as though it is a percussion instrument; the kōwhai in the spring and the pōhutukawa in the summer. One never fails to be moved by their beauty and uniqueness. The joy of the various flax flowers, with their distinct colours, is an abiding pleasure.'

There have been times over the past 25 years when nature has not cooperated. Rabbits and pūkeko are a nuisance. Frost-guard spray is essential, and she has to be vigilant for six months of the year: the earliest recorded frost they've had was on 28 March; the latest, on 2 November. Unreliable rainfall is a huge frustration. After a wet winter in 2017, summer drought came hot and heavy: they arrived back from Sydney to the worst drought in 20 years. 'It is heartbreaking,' Gillian says, 'but that's life, where we do not always have nature on our side.' She's had sleepless nights worrying about sickly griselinia, and how awful their green circles would look if some

Top left: Kahikatea, the native white pine (*Dacrycarpus dacrydioides*).
Top right: A line up of cabbage trees (*Cordyline australis*).
Bottom left: Neil Dawson's sculpture Feathersphere dances above the trees in this heavily planted gully.
Bottom right: A boardwalk in the wetlands.

died. Should she fill the gap with cabbage trees, even though cosseted, nursery-grown specimens of that size hate frost, uneven rainfall and fierce wind?

But despite such nightmares, Gillian is an optimist. Some garden areas have been planted several times — after figuring out what went wrong, she has another go. She says their late daughter Kristen taught her about serenity, which she has tried to capture in contemplative areas of the garden. Kristen was born with Rett syndrome: she gradually lost the power of speech and the ability to feed herself or to walk. 'But she still laughed and smiled and knew what was going on. Her spirit was amazing. She taught me patience and perseverance and to know always that the new morning light is a gift every day.'

The wetlands and native bush have been declared heritage areas by the Kapiti Coast District Council, and the Deanes recently arranged to have QEII National Trust covenants placed over four wetlands and native tree areas. Gillian's next big task — a massive undertaking — is to fell 12ha of mature pine trees and replace them with natives. 'The project is never-ending. I will happily work on it forever.' After all, she says, life is about adapting to changing circumstances — and plants are such good teachers.

Josie Martin
AKAROA

DELIGHT, JOY AND EXUBERANCE are writ large on the faces of visitors to The Giant's House garden in the French village of Akaroa, just outside Christchurch. It's heart-warming, says its creator, artist/gardener Josie Martin. In fact, it's her proudest achievement — transferring positive energy. The fact that people are smiling, dancing and singing makes her feel great, too. Quite often people are so moved they want to give her a hug; for most of them it seems to uplift their spirits. 'It's really wonderful if I'm doing something that I love that makes other people feel good.' Put another way, Josie has perfected the art of growing happiness.

After a spate of earthquakes in Canterbury, battered and emotionally bruised people came to linger awhile. 'People wanted to come to a happy place. That's special. I think, "Gosh, did I do that?"' And it's not just locals queuing at the gate: passengers from cruise ships, tourists and travellers all make a beeline for her playful garden.

It's hard not to get swept away once you're inside Josie's wonder world. Thanks to her mosaic artistry, it's peopled with cavorting acrobats, a pirate ship, a wood pigeon big enough to sit inside, a larger-than-life Marcel Marceau leaning on fresh air, and the Nosey Parkers, to name a few. And real flowers grow among them, climbing up bowers, filling out sculptures, glowing in the mixed border — not to forget the living statues of topiary. The real and surreal mix and mingle in one big happy garden party in the five-star garden of national significance.

A grand piano on the front lawn is rarely without a would-be concert pianist hamming it up to music broadcast through hidden speakers connected to Josie's iPad. The

Clockwise from top left: A forest of porcelain cones on stacked plates in a new area Josie calls Coniflora Galaxy. Nearby, at the entrance to the cafe, Flossie the Fat Lady is eating fresh strawberries instead of cupcakes; you reach the Bon Bon Palace by climbing the Rainbow Staircase lined with red cones of *Berberis thunbergii atropurpurea* 'Helmond Pillar' (and various people's heads); you're never alone in the Place des Amis.
Overleaf: Sinuous raised beds and hedges contain exuberant and colourful planting that lives in happy harmony with madcap mosaics.

succulents under its lid shimmer in the sunshine. 'People love the interaction,' says its inventor. Some sit there and play and sing along, especially French people for some reason. People dance and sing around it.

Josie says she couldn't have done this without her background in art and horticulture. 'Besides, I'm a bit of a workaholic and garden and art are my passion.' Everything you see in the garden now has gradually come together over 20 years, thanks to early morning gardening sessions before the gates open.

But Josie has always been driven. As a teenager, she worked a four-year apprenticeship at Wellington Botanic Garden while studying art at nights and weekends. She moved to Lincoln, where she continued her studies in horticulture, then grew cut flowers commercially for 16 years while raising three kids. 'It was pretty flat out,' she says. 'I had a big station wagon that I filled with flowers then had to get them to the airport by 8am. It was busy, but once the season ended I could paint the other three quarters of the year.' Seasonal work suits her down to the ground. 'But then I got a sore back and had to stop.' You wouldn't believe how heavy an armful of flowers can be, she says. She was devastated.

Time for a new direction. She searched for a small house with a big studio and found herself drawn to Akaroa, whose hills and coastal views recalled her childhood home of Wellington. 'I love the European feel to the place, too. I like being by the sea and Akaroa has a good climate. The soil I assumed would be okay because it's volcanic.' The rundown Victorian villa with good bones on Rue Balguerie that caught her eye was too big,

Clockwise from top left: The mime artist Marcel Marceau surveys the hills above Akaroa; black aeonium succulents ground the colourful setting for the Angel and Magician; cavorting acrobats in gymnastic poses by the lemon grove.
OVERLEAF
Top row from left: *Rosa* 'Leonardo da Vinci'; shaggy dinner-plate-sized yellow dahlia 'Encore'; Josie uses parsley everywhere.
Middle row from left: *Aeonium arboreum* 'Schwarzkopf'; the elegant canes of restio, *Elegia capensis*; Rudbeckia.
Bottom row from left: 'Katherine Mansfield' rose; Patio rose 'Scentasia'; 'Cerise' dahlia.
Opposite: The grand piano Sweet Patootie where succulents replace wires.

but it had potential — and the walls would be fantastic for hanging paintings. And for someone with an active imagination, this local legend about how the house got its name helped seal the deal. As Josie recounts in her book, *The Giant's House*, 'a little girl looked up in wonder at a grand house emerging from the bush above the settlement of Akaroa. "Giants live there," she said.'

Restoring the house left her short of cash for the garden but yielded buried treasure in the form of broken china, which she kept for a rainy day. As for the design, she made endless working drawings to see how the garden would flow with the form of the land. She knew she wanted colour, and that she wanted to integrate art into the garden.

Planting began near the house, and the rest happened organically. Josie's planting style is naturally unconventional — colour and texture, sweeps of succulents, natives and bright blooms, including a bank of 60 *Coleonema* 'Sunset Gold' above the mosaic clowns, are all swapped around frequently. It's pulled together by a soothing background of green lawns, shrubs and clipped hedges. Red poppies are mass-planted below a white wall of acrobats, and glossy black *Aeonium arboreum* 'Schwarzkopf' fill out a bed. Lashings of roses are either grouped in a single colour, mixed up in a patchwork of brights, or allowed to scramble over arbours.

Plants and sculpture exist as equals. 'I've been to a lot of sculpture gardens and felt they don't usually have a great connection between the two. But by putting plants inside the sculpture it makes a soft transition. The sculpture is not really an alien thing.' Initially Josie used powder-coated steel, but she was frustrated when the colours faded. Then

Top: Looking up to the Bon Bon Palace from the lawn by the house, across the rich tapestry of art and garden. Josie's world is inventive and intense and supremely cheerful.
Bottom: 'Leonardo da Vinci' roses planted en masse.

one day, while she was building a mosaic front step from that box of broken china, she realised that tiles keep their colour forever. The answer: get more tiles. She couldn't afford new, so she bought seconds, or rummaged and fossicked. And as word got out, boxes of tiles and china turned up at the gate, and people brought shards of precious china saved from quake-damaged homes. Imagine their bittersweet joy when they return to see their once-lost family treasure reborn as art.

Josie's life is still seasonal: she works like mad in spring and summer in the garden, then in winter she goes overseas, travelling and painting. Her kids are a major help, 'my best supporters'. Josie says her garden is like her diary; characters she has met on her travels pop up in mosaic form, outbuildings are done up in the style of a country she's visited. It's all out there. And it's all pretty happy.

Carolyn Ferraby
MARLBOROUGH

THERE'S A PHOTO OF CAROLYN FERRABY'S husband Joe asleep in a garden seat somewhere in the UK, a candid moment taken on holiday. The caption reads: 'One garden visit too many.' Carolyn tells this story with her trademark playful twinkle. Other times, she tells people that Joe thought he was marrying a wife; instead he got a gardener. Widen the lens and pull back and you'll see ample evidence at their farm in Marlborough that when florist met farmer, he supplied the biggest vase ever — and nearly 50 years on she's still having the time of her life arranging it.

Along the way Carolyn has rebelled against the property's name, Barewood, and created a luscious, fragrant, flower-crammed farm garden. Even the vegetable plot, a must when living 40 minutes from the nearest town of Blenheim, is an enviably beautiful French-style potager. Celebrated for her immaculate colour sense, she uses a florist's flair when choosing plants, laying down tone on tone as if in a watercolour painting. Rogue elements in the wrong livery get a quick heave-ho. Foliage is as important to the flower garden as it is to the vase, and she prides herself on growing complementary shrubs to fill out this dreamy scheme. She may live in a remote valley, one of the driest in New Zealand, but people attracted by stories of this elegant garden come to her by the coachload, up to 1000 a year, many from visiting cruise ships docked in Picton.

Others may open up their gardens for weddings, conferences or B&B guests, but Carolyn concentrates on welcoming garden lovers. She's determined that every season offers something deliciously different in the borders. It's still the thing she loves most:

Top: This hawthorn walk leads down to the summerhouses.
Bottom: What's a weeping willow without a pond? Joe answered that question with a digger and the result looks as pretty as a picture.
Overleaf: In a garden of extraordinary subtlety in which colour is nuanced rather than rowdy, this potager is a standout. Its high impact colour and intensive cultivation make it the envy — and ideal — of any gardener with a pulse. Bounded by a hedge of hornbeam, *Carpinus betulus*, when it comes to fruit, veges, herbs and flowers, what doesn't grow sideways grows up and over. Standardised *Ugni molinae*, or New Zealand cranberry, line the brick path, with two dark-leaved 'Samba' crab apples. The tunnel at the end features a heritage pear arch and nearby are heritage apple arches. 'My Castle' lupins and assorted poppies vie with sweet peas to be the brightest of them all.

'I feel very lucky. I can go out after breakfast and be there till dark.'

Excellence on this scale has its rewards. The New Zealand Gardens Trust has stamped Barewood a six-star garden of international significance. It's an accolade not given lightly, and for the owner, it's hard won — and even harder to maintain.

Carolyn says she's fortunate to have started the garden at a time when lots of plants were available, specialist local nurseries abounded and sourcing seed from England was still possible. She's always on the lookout for perennials that are interesting and different and finding a new one is a special moment. Lately she's been designing gardens for other people, which she says is a stimulating discipline, and tracking down plants for someone else has a useful spinoff for her own garden.

Carolyn is blessed with an acute visual memory. Her mother died when she was nine, but she says she could draw her garden now with every plant in it. Her mother was artistic, and she had a large picturesque garden at a time when there were few illustrated gardening books to inspire and inform.

When Carolyn and Joe took over the farm from his parents, she stood at the gate and visualised how it could be. They took the 100-year-old homestead back to its romantic best by knocking off a rather ugly modern sunroom and extending the verandah around the side — 'I wanted it dripping with old fashioned roses,' she says. Other ideas included revamping the existing vege plot behind the house, building a summerhouse up the back, and putting a hawthorn walk up there — because hawthorns are more appropriate than cherry trees in a farm

Clockwise from top left: Duck through hornbeam hedges from the side of the enclosed potager; colour co-ordinated giant red mustard and catnip make a pretty spring picture; old watering cans look decorative; cabbage, cavolo nero, poppies and Russell lupins in a tasty and tasteful display.

garden, she believes. They shifted the driveway so it doesn't cut the lawn in two, making a generous green entrance.

Carolyn devoured books: she learnt from the writings of 19th-century British designer Gertrude Jekyll that a garden should curtsey to the house, and Penelope Hobhouse taught her about plants. But the first and most memorable gardening book she read was on Sissinghurst Castle by English writer Anne Scott-James. When she visited the castle garden — the creation of Vita Sackville-West and her husband Harold Nicolson, and perhaps the most famous English garden of all — it lit a spark. I can do this, she thought, albeit on my own terms. And to keep the flame burning, she's returned five times to Sissinghurst.

In Marlborough Carolyn joined a local rhododendron society, which was a great learning curve; the best lesson was that she can't really grow them well at Barewood. But people were fantastically knowledgeable about all aspects of gardening and she soaked it all up. And, of course, she shared cuttings with other gardening-mad friends.

But what to do with clay soil? On the plus side, it stays moist in the summer, extending her growing season. But what can you plant that won't drown in winter, especially on the scale she envisaged? Joe helpfully softened it up with the farm gelignite until a better, less explosive, solution was found. Now she slathers the ground with trailerloads of sawdust, oak dross, pine needles and sheep manure plus handfuls of gypsum, and lets the worms do the work converting clay to friable loam. 'I can't *not* do that every year,' she says.

Looking back, she thinks she should have designed the garden on the page first, because

Top: One of two views of the flower draped verandah — from the inside you look out through a lacy fringe of white wisteria, a picture she had in her mind's eye from the start.
Bottom: Looking in from the sloping lawn in front, it's clear to see how Carolyn has softened the junction between house and paddock with a generous skirt of shrubbery.
OVERLEAF
Top: The summerhouse draped in roses ('Cressida', 'Desprez à Fleur Jaune') with shrub rose 'Ellen' in the foreground and to its right *Viburnum plicatum* 'Rosacea'.
Bottom: This beautiful perennial border shows Carolyn's verve with colour.
Facing page: The avenue of poplar trees leading from the front gates are *Populus nigra x euramericana* 'Crow's Nest'.

of course she's made a mistake or two — like the time they dug out a pond and realised they could not see it from the summerhouse. It might have been a disaster but visiting Australian designer Michael McCoy had a solution: bash through the wall. Hey presto, a water view revealed. But maybe a second summerhouse behind that one would tie it all together and make sense of the nascent orchard area behind. Done and done.

Carolyn and Joe often travel to visit great gardens, to look and learn, which keeps Carolyn's creative batteries fully charged — and Joe's flagging interest topped up by power naps. But this regime also lit a fuse back home. Why not celebrate the efforts of her local peers? There are great gardens at home, too . . . Carolyn and friends set up a festival of Marlborough gardens, which has grown steadily more popular every year: a quarter of a century later it draws 3000-plus tourists to the region for the four-day event.

They're also lured by the promise of rubbing shoulders with famous names in horticulture — for instance, Fergus Garrett, head gardener at the late Christopher Lloyd's masterpiece Great Dixter in the UK. For Carolyn, having Fergus to stay had specific benefits: he taught her how to prune her newly established orchard. 'There's work to be done there,' she says happily.

A less task-oriented visitor left a lasting impression too. Cruise-ship passengers usually come for the outing, a chance to stretch their sea legs and explore the countryside. But occasionally, says Carolyn, 'I get a gardener' — such as the attentive Frenchman who followed her around Barewood, kissing her hand. 'C'est magnifique,' he insisted, speaking in a language we understand.

Sally Woodham
HAWKES BAY

IF YOU GARDEN FOR LONG ENOUGH you create your own individual style. Take Sally Woodham in Haumoana, halfway between Hastings and Napier in Hawkes Bay. She remembers very clearly the day husband John made the unexpected winning bid for a 4ha block of land. She says it's the best thing that ever happened because, in the 40 years since then, she has created an exciting original garden — though she's the last one to brag.

The idea was to raise their three children on a lifestyle block and grow fruit. Their small orchard produced kiwifruit, citrus, apples and rockmelons with varying degrees of success. Then Sally began to focus on the garden. 'There wasn't a lot of planning going on here — more what John would describe as "a Mrs Plonk exercise".' When the chooks and pigs down by the creek were moved on, she set to with a spade, digging out her first garden bed by hand. That's where she planted heritage roses in the cottage style of the time. But where Sally saw their beauty, John saw red — and thorns, which made his hedge trimming a prickly nightmare. 'He modified their romantic and sweet-sounding names to incorporate some coarse and blasphemous alternatives,' says Sally.

You could never describe a cottage garden as easy-care, especially for this busy mother working fulltime as a physiotherapist. So Sally started to experiment with design. She changed the overall structure of the garden with hedges and upright evergreens, and worked with the seasons. The roses largely disappeared, making way for perennial and herbaceous borders and colour-themed areas.

Luckily there's plenty of water — with a bore and a creek — good loamy silt deposits

Clockwise from top left: This water feature matured from a broken red chair to a stylish focal point showcasing bromeliads; curious cacti and succulents start off in a miniature garden on the kitchen bench; hard to miss the front door with its towering cacti, ideal for the dry growing conditions in Hawkes Bay.
Overleaf: Prepare to be dazzled — blue *Agave americana* and orange-flowering *Aloe variegata* near the driveway.

from the nearby Tukituki River, and great weather — except for the wind: Haumoana translates as 'strong wind from the sea'. But they managed this by planting a background perimeter hedge of tall, dense Leyland cypress (*Cupressus leylandii*).

When Sally joined a gardening club, it was the start of something wonderful. She met experienced and knowledgeable gardeners who were generous to newcomers. It's there that she made friends with like-minded newbie, orchardist Julie Russell (meet Julie on page 108) and the two have encouraged each other ever since. What with club events, travel, reading, 'and necessity', Sally developed the skills and confidence to empower her own efforts. She still doesn't know the names of plants, but that doesn't hold her back. 'Names of plants are not a high priority,' she says. 'Who they came from, their different forms, effects and combinations are far more important to me.'

When the Woodhams replaced their old cottage in 1996 with a new house designed by John, Sally set out to match its quirky modernity with a fresh style of garden at the front of the property. Here cacti, succulents, orchids, palms and their spiky friends and family rule. Avenues of agaves and aloes, islands of statuesque cacti, a sunken gravel garden of succulents, cacti and bromeliads, and groups of orchids, are displayed with aplomb — and they're pretty low-maintenance, too. She took inspiration from a book about Jacques Majorelle, a French artist whose finest work is his famous garden in Morocco.

Sally has coveted these plants since she was a girl, inspired by her grandma in Dannevirke, but they're hard to find locally. 'I'm always

Top: The original cottage site lives again as a classy outdoor eating area with flourishing crucifix orchids and cacti.
Bottom: Sally's round lawn which acts as a meeting point for the old and new areas of the garden.

on the lookout and source them from all over,' she says. 'I pounce when I see a plant I must have.' The furthest and craziest sortie? Driving to Matakana and back in one day for a load of bromeliads, a round trip of 900km — that's 13 hours of driving, door to door. But you couldn't find them in garden centres in those days, she explains.

Designwise, connecting the new to the more established existing garden proved a challenge. The solution is a sunken round lawn outlined by hedges of *Picea glauca,* buxus and rosemary. This area acts as a pause between the architectural forms at the front and the lush beds of the more traditional shrubs and flowers at the back. Think of the whole garden as Sally's personal timeline of maturity, where different design styles coexist, thanks to her skill. Emotionally, its impact is dramatic and romantic in equal measure.

Boundaries seem to disappear in their inside/outside house. Indoors, views of the garden can be seen from every vantage point, and people and plants live together on an almost equal footing. There are table displays here, dramatic potted specimens there. In the kitchen, crockery jostles for counter space with madly exotic plants, and the living room is festooned with a striking collection of mature orchids in bowls of John's design.

Not surprisingly, Sally dreams of having a conservatory where she can grow subtropical plants that struggle in the Hawkes Bay climate. 'I've got tremendous plans . . . I could potter there to my heart's content when it's raining. All the crucifix orchids have to be put under cover in winter anyway: we get enough frosts to do damage.'

Every gardener needs an enabler. Sally's John is the guy who's created one-of-a-kind

Top row from left: Flower of the hairy old man cactus *Cephalocereus senilis*; *Hydrangea macrophylla* 'Merveille Sanguine' (or 'Bloody Marvellous'); one of the many crucifix orchids Sally treasures.
Middle row from left: *Aloe polyphylla* from Lesotho; the spiny *Euphorbia polygona*; the century plant *Agave americana*.
Bottom row from left: Detail of an aloe flower; Bernie's dahlia named after its donor; avocados.

planters by ingeniously recycling everyday throwaways such as stainless-steel washing machine drums. A fountain presiding over the sunken gravel garden, which is the focal point for the deck and living areas, was fashioned from a stylish red dining chair (not that you'd know it by looking). He's turned galvanised painter's trestles into a romantic arbour for climbers. His sculptures can be seen wherever you look.

And when Sally complained about annoyingly wonky trolleys at garden centres, he invented a better one, sparking a new business venture: his trolleys can now be seen smoothly trundling through garden centres around the world. Sally had to wait a long time to get her own version, but it's her favourite gardening tool now — of course.

Kath Irvine
OHAU

YOU CAN TELL SOMEONE EXCELS at gardening when her larder is bulging. Kath Irvine grows so much produce on her 0.4ha Ohau smallholding near Levin that she struggles to invent nifty ways to preserve it all. She loves to grow things, it's what occupies her thoughts all the time, she says. Inspired by permaculture, she's created beauty and bounty from an unpromising patch of rocks and bog — and a garden that looks good enough to eat.

Kath also makes a living from her food garden in the wop wops. She runs workshops for kitchen gardeners and permaculture beginners, consults privately, gives talks, runs community ventures, and designs and troubleshoots other people's plots. She worked for years as a green gardener for the local council in Kapiti, offering advice on sustainable growing methods. And in the little red caravan beyond the orchard, after a day outside, she slips off gumboots and gardening gloves and settles in behind her laptop to tend a growing network of fans who relish postings and how-to books from her website, Kath Irvine's Edible Backyard.

Kath says it all started with eczema: she had a 'shocking' case of it as a child, and had to stay covered up and smothered in creams. By the age of 16 she'd discovered that chemicals were her trigger, and that a regime of eating brown rice and drinking cider vinegar helped. After a while her skin cleared up and to her great delight, people didn't recognise her with her clear complexion. She quit her office job and travelled the country, meeting people who lived off the land. She felt 'an instant connection . . . I loved that people were working to feed their kids well, that they were growing it all. I loved the camaraderie of it.'

Nowadays she's a poster girl for the health-

Clockwise from top left: A wildflower corner with borage and poppies to lure bees and brighten up the work area; Kath composts in small lots as she weeds, covering them with old bags that once contained wool, to speed decomposition; Intensive cultivation is only possible in rich friable soil.
Overleaf: This curving rock wall has rustic charm, but it also demonstrates Kath's thrifty wisdom. Before she could start growing anything, she dug up barrow-loads of rocks which she recycled. Her curving garden wall divider not only looks attractive, it absorbs heat by day and blesses nearby crops with its stored warmth at night.

giving vitality of homegrown food and the physical effort that raising such produce demands. When she and her sawmiller partner Matt found this land a decade ago their priorities were: reliable water supply (it's a high rainfall area, with gravity-fed springs from the hills), beneficial growing conditions (the hills shelter them from the worst winds), and an old house they could do up. 'I wasn't worried about the soil. I knew if it wasn't greywacke I could improve it.' And it was cheap, too. There was just one drawback: the earth was full of rocks.

Matt built temporary raised beds to get her started, while Kath tackled the ground. You could say her first harvest was walls, built one levered-out rock at a time. Creating good friable soil out of what was left was a challenge, she admits, but all it took was graft, lots of compost and patience — and her favourite tool, the broadfork, a garden aerator (that's what Kath's using in her portrait on page 79). 'The broadfork is the best tool ever — though surprisingly old-fashioned,' she says. Its job is to aerate and open up soil. 'Healthy soil needs 50 per cent air, so for anyone on a clay base it's an essential tool. Opening the soil up with those long tines not only gets air in to keep soil healthy, it allows roots to go straight down instead of sideways, where they compete. You can plant veges closer this way.'

For pure joy she swears by flower power, the bees, the parasitic wasps and the lacewings too: 'For the magic they bring, the quiet power they wield.' Come spring in the potager, Kath scatters flower seed among the veges 'to create some wild, carefree beauty' — anise, hyssop, echium, larkspur, calendula, chamomile, snapdragon, stock, heartsease, poppies, love-in-a-mist, honeywort, sweetpeas and hollyhocks.

Clockwise from top left: Lupin seeds about to be sown for a green crop to enrich the soil; Kath grows her tender seedlings in the greenhouse; such rich soil is the result of careful permaculture practice; Wyandotte chickens play a vital role in the garden.

Down in the greenhouse, which is essential for extending the short growing season, there's a warm place for tomatoes and aubergines that would turn up their toes outside. Then there's the berry house that keeps the fruit unmolested from roaming critters.

In the orchard, after a serious sampling exercise, Kath chose to plant 'Luisa', 'Omega', 'Tamaki' and 'Hawera' plums because she likes their flavours, fresh, bottled or dried. Maybe a smaller orchard would be sensible, now her four kids are growing up, she wonders. 'Maybe if I was starting again I'd have more grazing.' Grow less? Who's she kidding! What's needed right now is a good-sized cool store, something more reliable than the old fridge in the shed, where individually wrapped fruit is kept at 4–6°C to stop the rot and thwart rats. 'My preference is to have something electricity-free — a pātaka (raised storehouse) or some such.'

Chickens range freely, within limits: her clucking clouds of Shavers, Wyandottes and Light Sussex are fenced in a paddock away from temptation in the garden. They play their part in the food chain by keeping designated weeds down, depositing manure and producing eggs and, at the end of a long and useful life, giving their all for the Sunday boil-up. Even the oldest campaigners have an afterlife: Kath buries them wherever she's developing a new area.

Kath says her proudest moment came in year three when, for the first time, she grew all their veges. Favourites in winter are leeks, Romanesco broccoli, celery, parsnips, Brussels sprouts and yams. Come spring, it'll be asparagus and artichokes. That's when the garden is a jungle of hollyhocks, bishop's flower (*Ammi majus*), echinacea, dahlias and *Verbena bonariensis.* It's whimsical and pretty,

Top row from left: *Phacelia tanacetifolia*, purple tansy; buckwheat *Fagospyrum esculentum*; perennial statice has long-lasting flowers.
Middle row from left: Summer salad greens; peg wet gloves out to dry and to keep track of them; Moira poppy, named after a friend who gave Kath the seeds.
Bottom row from left: Bee-friendly borage; flowering mustard; the long stems of 'Purple King' lavender.

and tall enough to disappear into. She mixes different lettuce seeds in a bowl then scatters them about to grow close together, which keeps the weeds out. The main herbs are parsley, borage, lemon balm, comfrey, yarrow, pineapple sage, chamomile and chicory.

Growing your own food is not that hard, she insists. It's seven days a week but she loves it. And being a naturally speedy person and having been a gardener for a long time, she can get a lot done fast. 'I look forward to slow gardening, doodling about a bit more as responsibilities subside. I've got a few replacements to ponder — the goat ate the apricot tree and there's a pear with fireblight, and I would love to grow a maple to harvest the syrup . . .'

Jo Beetham
WAIRARAPA

LESS GARDEN EQUALS MORE JOY. Not that Jo Beetham dislikes gardening — far from it, but she's learned to keep it manageable to ensure peace of mind and to spare her body. She says she's a half-hearted gardener now, which, looking at her property overlooking the Gladstone Valley in the Wairarapa, you can take with a pinch of salt.

The edgy contemporary architecture of the house is matched in mood and form by a fringe of native planting that melts seamlessly into the wider landscape. It's an understated, seemingly simple garden, but much thought and planning has gone into tying house to land.

Compared with her last garden, this one is a doddle to run and that's just what she wanted. The English-style country garden that she nurtured for 36 years was 'rather large', with traditional mixed herbaceous borders. Lots of *Alchemilla mollis*, acanthus, iris, drifts of catmint for miles . . . you get the picture. And despite the fact she raised three children and worked full time in her own physiotherapy practice in Masterton, she did it all herself.

It was a reprieve from a stressful job, she says. As well as the million other tasks this energetic farmer's wife could fit into her day: breeding ostriches, selling loo seats . . . pardon, what? They were Perspex with barbed wire inside, she explains; very arty. And for three years she was the local agent for fashion designer Trish Gregory. But gradually the urge grew to simplify, downsize, start afresh. Jo wanted another type of garden, one that she could manage easily, but just as importantly, it should be a place that would satisfy a need in her creative soul.

Jo's husband Mont is a fifth-generation farmer on land his family has owned since

Clockwise from top left: A close up of Phil Price's sculpture Kiss; Jeff Thomson's iron dogs guard the entrance; flax flowers, a ready source of blooms for Jo's giant outdoor vase; jazzy herb containers which the cook can reach through the kitchen window.
Overleaf: Bookend walls echo living shelterbelts further down the hill, while the garden, consisting of only slightly tamed native plants, meets the landscape in a seamless composition. Now that's how to do a low maintenance garden.

1846. They lived in Kouarau, a century-old, romantic-style French-accented wooden mansion that boasted seven bedrooms, a billiard room and wide verandahs. Gorgeous, of course, but not surprisingly it was a demon to heat — and to maintain.

One fateful day, says Jo, Mont was painting their 600-square-metre home when he reckoned this was his fifth go at it. Jo had been keen to move for a while, not just to downsize but for the creative challenge. Sensing a fertile moment to suggest an alternative, 'I pounced,' she says. And in the fullness of time they upped sticks.

The Beethams' new property is just 3km away, on the edge of an escarpment and with amazingly wide rural views and an everchanging sky. Here Australian architect Graham Fisher created a strong-minded house that some call brutalist — but not Jo.

Masculine is her word for it. And look, she points out, see the way its squared-off, bookend walls echo the shape of those rural shelterbelts? Its form echoes the landscape.

When you drive through the gap in the first 8m x 25m wall, you enter a courtyard where all is quiet in the lee of the wind. A pair of dog sculptures by Jeff Thomson guards the front door. And as you turn around you start to notice the garden, which takes up only a smidgeon of the property's 4.5ha — and how it's deliberately kept at arm's length from the house.

Jo called on Masterton garden designer Lyn Eglinton of Stablehouse Design (meet Lyn on page 222) to help her make the move from traditional to minimal. 'She did a sketch,' says Jo, 'and we talked about texture with mass-planting.' As she explains: 'You must look to the future, to your mobility. Nowadays

Top: At the top of the slope, muehlenbeckia humps and mounds define the edge of the house lawn. Jo and Mont swear it takes them next to no time to trim them. The yellow artwork, Kiss, is by sculptor Phil Price.
Bottom: Mont gets a stirring view of the Wairarapa countryside while mowing pathways through the flax and grasses.

I'd be a nutcase to have perennials and a herbaceous border.'

Lyn suggested starting with four plants — *Muehlenbeckia astonii, Laurus nobilis, Anemanthele lessoniana* and, for the courtyard bank, *Arthropodium cirratum*. And only the latter — the rengarenga lilies — have disappointed. The snails love them to death, so Jo is gradually replacing them with *Hedera canariensis*. 'Everyone tells me the ivy will kill all the trees, but I like the big glossy leaf, so I'm prepared to watch it carefully.'

Putting the plan into action was a huge exercise, says Jo. But first, they had to make their dense clay soil plant-friendly by folding in 'mountains of gypsum' using a huge grader, rather like a giant cake mixer. Everything was bought in multiples: 200 rengarenga to a bed; 500 muehlenbeckia here and so on.

At the front, the garden begins beyond the lawn, on the lip of the escarpment. That's where muehlenbeckia flourish, clipped into artful rambling shapes by Mont three or four times a year. 'It only takes half a day,' says Jo. Further down the slope, flax and cabbage trees take over the job of filtering the wind. And in the gullies beyond, they planted kānuka, tōtara and five fingers. The subsequent explosion in bird life is a total joy for Jo: it's proof they're loving the new garden as much as its human owners do.

On the northern side, Jo installed an orchard of 25 fruit trees, including a citrus grove, and fig trees that are allowed free rein to flourish in a paddock. 'I've got seven different fig varieties. I love their look and I'm allowing them to get huge. We have a three-month fig season from February and I give most of the fruit away.'

She's also growing sunny yellow

Top row from left: Kōwhai fronds *Sophora molloyii* 'Dragon's Gold'; *Anemanthele lessoniana*; oioi, *Apodasmia similis*.
Middle row from left: Kanuka *Kunzea ericoides*; grapefruit harvest; *Hedera canariensis*.
Bottom row from left: Rampant rhubarb; titoki *Alectryon excelsus*; *Muehlenbeckia astonii*.

tamarillos. Mont grows their veges, so they're self-sufficient in everything but flowers . . . which are where, by the way? The closest thing you'll find to a floral display is a clever, larger than life, artful installation outside the kitchen window. Mounted on a concrete plinth is a gigantic clay pot that Jo fills with flax stems. 'I like to think it's a vase of flowers on the table,' she says with a grin.

For Jo, the last garden drove her. Been there, done that: with this one, she's firmly in the driving seat. Now, having sold her business she is happy getting her hands dirty restoring a classic 1954 Ferguson tractor in the garage. And there's always another arts initiative to get her fundraising juices running. Plus, she's on the roster for Victim Support. Just as well her new garden is so biddable.

Loena McCormack
AUCKLAND

AUCKLAND TEACHER LOENA McCORMACK'S pared-back approach to gardening has produced real drama and she couldn't be happier. The lesson learned here in the historic seaside suburb of Mission Bay is that the future of gardening is shrinking — but in a good way. At Loena's place you can walk across her rear courtyard in three steps, from dining room to boundary water feature. Her front patio is equally pocket-sized. Yet each area packs a punch well above its fighting weight. Together they add up to a visionary prototype for gardeners whose ardour for their hobby remains undimmed, though their energy and reach may have diminished. And it's a compelling case study in living on shrinking sections, as cities become more densely populated.

Loena's place distils the essence of inspired gardening without sacrificing swagger or the element of surprise. It's like a tropical terrarium, a miniature world of lush leaf forms in every shade of green. And it's all grown in containers. 'I've always liked that tropical feel,' she says. During her teacher training years she spent the long summer holidays travelling, mostly around the Pacific Islands. In those days she sported a year-round tan, carefully burnished on beach vacations — until a dose of melanoma changed her ways forever. Recovered from her fright, she now wears hats with great flair, belying their serious intent. But an addiction to jungly flora stuck.

Loena's first garden in Mt Eden boasted two huge old kentia palms (*Howea forsteriana*), underplanted with tropical-looking vireya rhododendrons and black taro. 'I couldn't believe how things grew in that volcanic soil,' she says. When she downsized to this 1970s

Top: In the top garden, terracing in a tight space allows plants and sculpture their moment in the spotlight.
Bottom: Near the Corten steel fence is a spiral seashell sculpture by one of her pupils Clint Slogrove.
Overleaf: In this tiny courtyard that makes a massive statement using colour and simple planting, the stage is set for drama.

townhouse she brought plants and cuttings, hoping to recreate another patch of Pasifika. But disaster struck. A giant ponga tree fern replanted with care turned up its toes in a few days. 'When I dug it out I discovered the whole garden was a clay pan.'

Help was at hand. A successful collaboration with garden designer Trish Bartleet and her architect husband Mal that had begun in Mt Eden was reconvened in Mission Bay. The soil problem was solved by ignoring it and instead building deep concrete planter boxes: filled with good container mix and nourished frequently with a high-voltage fertiliser, they house a hedge-like row of Costa Rica bamboo palms (*Chamaedorea costaricana*). On the deck, four different varieties of slow-growing cycad gently simmer in pots. Heads of black taro nod hello. The sibilant murmur of water in the red glass fountain focuses the mind on the here and now; there had been talk of building an outdoor fireplace, but Loena wanted the tranquil sight and sound of running water instead. When the mood takes her, she unfurls a tribal rug, sets out a couple of classy chairs and a crocodile-shaped table, points the remote at her awning and settles down with a book. And after dark, when the lights come on, you could almost be at the theatre waiting for the drama to unfold.

It's a family trait. Loena's mother was a keen member of her hometown drama club in Putaruru, where her daughter was enlisted to paint backdrops, stitch on buttons or stick feathers on hessian. Boring, thought little Loena. 'But it must have had some impact because I go to live theatre every Saturday night. And it might perhaps explain how I'm always staging things in the garden, moving pots around.' It helps explain her delightful

Clockwise from top left: A haunting face by Nicky Jolly hosts the delicate trailing succulent *Sedum morganianum* aka donkey tail, with *Vriesea fosteriana rubra* in the foreground; Loena revved up the café setting with her trademark red paint and served up a bowl of bromeliads to match; ceramicist Susan St Lawrence created the torso (and the giant foot seen elsewhere), a perfect foil for this group of potted cycad, hoya and palm; palm fronds reflected in the bird bath by ceramicist Phillip Luxton.

name too, which she shares with her aunt and with the courtesan in Offenbach's opera *La Belle Hélène*.

Sitting out by the fountain is very therapeutic, she says . . . but it doesn't always last. Loena gets gardener's itch, 'because the garden is just a few metres from the door and living areas, so I have to look after it as well as the interior,' she explains. It's a little more labour-intensive than she imagined. At the weekends, she'll spend about an hour grooming the palms; their fronds get sunburned in summer and their bamboo-like stems produce husks that often need combing out.

From her kitchen sink Loena looks down on a stream, home to blue-cheese-loving eels (she feeds them, and knows their taste). She fenced its boundaries for peace of mind and built a bridge to reach marginal plants and a ledge full of pots. 'On the map it's an easement, but really it's a glorified drain, though it begins life as a river.'

Flower lovers might notice a lack of blooms in her garden, but Loena says she can always buy a bunch down the road. The second patio, below the front fence — a controversial choice for neighbours, who wondered why she'd chosen rusty (Corten) steel — houses spiky plants. Sadly, gravel does not deter slugs and snails, so she's thinking of replacing it with bark, to encourage the aloes, bromeliads, succulents and cacti to flourish.

But Loena's garden is mostly a low-maintenance, all-seasons proposition. 'I want to enjoy my garden without being panicked into having to do something according to the calendar. I'd like to be more methodical, but life is busy . . .'

If she ever gets sick of teaching English, she

Top row from left: The statuesque dune aloe, *Aloe thraskii*; seeds from the bamboo lookalike palm *Chamaedorea costaricana*; *Monstera deliciosa* grows indoors and out. **Middle row from left:** Ornamental taro; 'Blue Sky' echeveria; *Vriesea splendens* 'Flaming Sword'. **Bottom row from left:** *Vriesea fosteriana* 'Rubra'; *Libertia ixioides* 'Goldfinger'; *Aloe polyphylla*.

could give seminars on container planting. She prefers pots that blend with the natural environment rather than ones that shout for individual attention. Two large handmade pots, bought while she was at university 'for an arm and a leg, and a bit more', taught her an invaluable trick. She'd left palms growing in them for too long and their roots had grown into the clay. She tried cutting them out, but the knife would only go down so far. Pulling didn't work. Then she spotted her water blaster: why not try to blast them out? It worked a charm. But always remember to dress accordingly and wear goggles, she advises ruefully.

Nowadays, she says, 'As I've got older and not quite so strong, any time I want to repot something I roll the container on its side and use the water blaster.' From small places, big ideas can grow.

Julie Russell
HAWKES BAY

THE BEST GARDENS AGE LIKE FINE WINE. A first encounter with Round Pond in Bridge Pā, Hawkes Bay revealed a garden with a rosy glow: at just 10 years old it felt confident, if not yet complete. Even then it swept you up into its vast prettiness — it almost shimmered in the heat, alive with designer touches, delighting with its contrast between the agricultural and the domestic.

A decade or so on and it's matured into a fine drop. The distant views of Te Mata Peak and Mt Erin still draw the eye, but the garden is now the stronger magnet, bursting with fresh and artful colour compositions. Each area of excellence in this 4ha spread leads gently to the next. Julie Russell has chosen every plant, shrub and tree and given them all room to flourish. You can tell her favourites are buxus: she has thousands of them, raised by her own fair hands. Start with a sugarloaf hill padded with nearly 3000 buxus plants, presided over by a goat. Just over there, a crowd of 600 or so green shrubs shaped like people, and check out the shallow inverted buxus maze interplanted with lychnis (rose campion). Everywhere you look, count the soft round balls of buxus topiary.

The large circular pond with dancing waterworks stars front of house, especially when spotlit on a velvet-dark summer's night. Nearer the house there's a tiled, Persian-inspired kitchen courtyard. Julie's extensive, mainly pink double border around the back is a patchwork of complementary colours, and on the other side of the house, a rill alongside an elegant pergola reflects the sky. Industrial containers rescued from the now defunct Tomoana freezing works near Hastings are reborn as stylish raised beds and given the Julie treatment with herbs and flowers.

Top: Wildflowers grown on this scale every two years – it's a gigantic task that Julie relishes for the sheer delight of sowing beauty that's also a bright backdrop for art.
Bottom: The round pond on a summer's night, with the wildflowers beyond.
Overleaf: A horse sculpture by Philipp Meier finds a temporary billet in this part of the garden where Julie has worked her magic turning cypress and olive trees into natural works of art.

There's even a secret sculpture garden dedicated to her helpers. 'I enjoy a bit of whimsy,' she says.

And every two years, Julie and husband Mike excavate a half-hectare paddock and seed it with wildflowers to provide a colourful setting for the sale of outdoor sculpture. This hospice fundraiser is one of the few times Round Pond is open to the public. 'You need to keep stretching,' she explains. 'And we really enjoy having people here.' Plus, it's their way of contributing to charity and giving artists exposure. This way, she makes a concentrated effort to prepare for the public and, after a couple of weeks, it's all over; she and Mike and their helpful posse of family and friends can relax and enjoy their work in peace.

It's a huge commitment keeping Round Pond looking amazing. But Julie relishes a challenge. She inherited her father's Presbyterian work ethic, loves growing things and was fortunate enough to marry a man who 'puts up with this madness. Not many men could do it, I have to admit.' Mike is her keenest helper. 'We live and breathe this place. We're crazy together.'

They met when Julie was an arts graduate who gravitated to marketing in the plant nursery business, and Mike was a fruit grower. They married and settled down to grow fruit commercially and raise a family. Julie also grew and sold dried flowers and, later, fresh flowers from home. 'And I started growing buxus from cuttings, and lonicera, some of which we sold.' She developed a garden with borders and a rockery. When they decided to buy a bigger block of land across the road to create a new house and garden from scratch, she stopped selling the seedlings and instead grew them for her own plot. A friend drew up an outline plan for the garden, indicating

Top row from left: Lavender-toned delphinium; this striped dahlia was a gift from a friend; yellow knapweed *Centaurea macrocephala*.
Middle row from left: Hot pink cactus dahlia; Soldier and Shirley poppies; pink peony also given by a friend.
Bottom row from left: *Rosa* 'Emily'; new spring foliage of buxus; 'Fourth of July' climbing rose.

planting areas. 'When we came over here we had buxus, lonicera and small sticks of trees. Plus we put in Italian alders around the property to give us structure and protect us from the wind.'

That was in 1994, the year hail wrecked many orchards right on picking time — including theirs. 'Hundreds of bins of fruit about to be picked, our flower crop that was completely shredded, and the garden . . . which took some time to recover.' It was her saddest moment, but they carried on and are still successfully growing plums.

At first Julie was mad about English gardening, perennial borders, à la Gertrude Jekyll. 'It took me a long time to realise I could not do an English border in this dry, almost Mediterranean climate.' Adapting her vision to reality, she incorporated flowers that thrive in the dry summers: salvias, *Phlomis russeliana* (Jerusalem sage), sedum, euphorbia and geraniums. She loves the way the red border with cannas, berberis and day lilies strobes in the bright sunshine. Trees that thrive here include oaks, *Arbutus unedo* (the strawberry tree), loquats and 200 olives. What makes the garden so distinctive, she says, is having the green everywhere, with the brights. 'We had 65 people here for a barbecue recently and, someone remarked that it looks like an oasis.'

In her early days as a gardener, Julie's confidence grew exponentially after she joined Hortus, a local club. Visiting other people's gardens and learning from their experience was an incredible boost. And she found a kindred spirit in another new member, Sally Woodham from nearby Haumoana (meet Sally on page 68). 'Sally and I were the youngest and the least experienced. We were much the same

Left: The mature zigzagging juniper hedge marks the boundary between garden and plum orchard while sheltering this corner where Julie has shaped bay trees into something special.

PREVIOUS PAGE
Top left: Te Mata Peak and Mt Erin, seen through the limbed up mature hedge trees, find their echo in curvy clipped hedges.
Bottom left: In this shady picnic area a plantation of hydrangeas takes colour cues from the peeling bark of *Acer griseum*.
Top right: The resplendent pink perennial double border, where topiary lends weight to a changing display of flowers, is anchored by the painted wall behind.
Bottom right: Julie's maze winds down into the earth, as a counterpoint to her nearby buxus hill. Here white feathery *Lychnis coronaria* lightens the clipped spiral buxus hedge that leads to a sculpture by Paul Beaurepaire.

age, with babies the same age. We felt way out of our league so we kind of held hands. Sally and I are friends for life. We've supported each other to keep going and keep looking. Most people don't understand such passion,' she says. The friends have kept themselves inspired by visiting gardens and garden centres all over the country, attending design conferences and checking out celebrated gardens overseas. A course given by Sir Miles Warren was another boost for Julie. 'He started Ohinetahi, his second garden, at 40, just like I did here,' she says.

Julie's favourite overseas garden is La Louve, an elegant, understated hillside property in Provence created by former Hermès designer Nicole de Vésian, where 'everything is so beautifully crafted'. She's now planting a new garden area around the back, inspired by de Vésian's.

Change is a mantra in Julie's world as she strives to create a perfect picture. 'It's a constant task to balance shapes, volumes, textures and colours. The garden needs to work looking at it from different angles. To make the gardens blend successfully so they all work together is a challenge and it is an art.'

Don't tell her it all looks like too much work. 'It annoys me when people say that. I quite like all this topiary and we only cut it once a year.' After all, she explains, this garden is for her and her family and friends.

As for the future, 'We'll stay here as long as we can. It's my passion and my love. I tend not to worry too much about the future. If it never comes to anything else after I'm gone then that's what it is.'

Sarah Caughley
WELLINGTON

CREATING AN ELEGANT COURTYARD GARDEN in Wellington is a coup — especially for someone who hates gardening in the wind. The capital city is defined by its blustery squalls; but on a good day it's hard to beat this place for stunning views of harbourside and hills. As for accessible flat ground around the house, it's a luxury for a green-fingered Wellingtonian. But if anyone could pull it off, it's garden designer Sarah Caughley.

When Sarah first moved to Wellington it took her a while to accept that she wasn't living in the country anymore, and that, though the house had a charming country feel, it came with next to no garden.

Sarah was raised on a farm in Okareka near Rotorua, where she used to 'run around the paddocks all day like a sheepdog'. She had worked in garden centres before she married Richard and moved to the city. Energetic and creative, she pined for a project — until their three children came along and she started enjoying city life. And once the feverish clamour of babyhood calmed to a dull roar, she went back to work in a garden centre. There she learned which plants were suitable for the capital's climate, and a two-year course in landscape design taught her how to use them.

Ten years or so after moving to the house in Wadestown, Sarah found the time to get serious about her section. They bought the neighbouring property so they could remove a massive clay bank that loomed over one side of the house: this involved trucking 160 loads of clay up a steep slope in a narrow street in a major gear-grinding exercise. Sarah planted the newly built raised garden and its paved terrace, but this exercise ended abruptly when her vegetables took flight in the wind: gusts of 120kph sent even the outdoor

Previous page: The crooked plum tree with potted succulent and glossy *Ligularia reniformis* makes an artful installation in the original side garden.
Top: Sarah kept the new courtyard open and elegant by using simple shapes for her topiary.
Bottom: Before the trees grew into a shelter 'belt' at the far end, plants and furniture were bowled like skittles.

furniture skittling. That bulky old bank had at least provided some shelter; in its absence the wind whipped around unchecked.

Undaunted, Sarah grew a windbreak below the terrace, using a foolproof selection of wind-tolerant plants such as karo, ngaio, lonicera, English and Portuguese laurel, *Viburnum japonicum,* the griselinias littoralis and lucida, corokia and *Coprosma repens,* lots of miniature toetoe (*Chionochloa flavicans*) and rengarenga lilies (*Arthropodium cirratum*). (Take care to plant everything securely in the ground, Sarah cautions, to avoid wind-rock.) *Tecomanthe speciosa* weaves between the branches, filling in the gaps. Once they all began to thrive, Sarah had another go at the terrace.

The original idea for an edible parterre was shelved because of the wind and the wind-chill factor. Growing all her own food — the most intensive form of gardening, which requires daily attendance — proved impossible when the wind chased her back indoors. Instead Sarah has surrounded her fountain with plumptious cubes of *Corokia virgata* 'Geenty's Green'. The raised boundary beds house topiaried shrubs, tree ferns and flax, large standard acmenas, the occasional rose, hydrangeas, lavender and buxus, siren-red pelargoniums, and a fenceline shrouded in climbers. And beside the house, shabby chic containers of buxus and succulents and a hedge of bulletproof Indian hawthorn (*Rhaphiolepis indica*) soften the junction where weatherboard meets paving.

Around the other side of the house, a soft carpet of lawn surrounded by buxus-edged beds is presided over by a splendid old cabbage tree and an Irish yew Sarah planted the year her daughter Rachael was born. The plum is

Clockwise from top left: The windy front end, now a study in layered planting; buxus hedging; Sarah deliberately screens fences for a more spacious feel; stately pots lend distinction to buxus.

a favourite: she rescued it from the diggers and dragged it around the house to its new spot here opposite the dining-room window. A 100-year-old white flowering *Camellia japonica* and a *Magnolia soulangeana*, which she inherited with the house, have earned Sarah's respect and affection. But perhaps her favourite part of the garden is a patch of wild grass nodding in the breeze, a little touch of country she can't live without.

Sarah describes herself as a frugal gardener. 'I try to be economical,' she says. 'I'd rather spend the money going somewhere warm in the winter.' She trawls the sick bays in garden centres and nurseries, looking for patients she can nurse back to health (don't be afraid to unravel the roots, is her tip). Lavender, rosemary and hydrangeas are all grown from cuttings. She grows succulents for containers and groundcover because they're biddable.

Patience is a big money saver, too, says Sarah. Buy small plants and wait for them to grow instead of going for an instant effect with larger, more expensive plants.

Not one to coddle, she swears by choosing the right plant for the place. Clay and rock? She takes what she gets and deals with it, without using imported soil. There's no need to feed or fertilise, she says, because plants don't need a lot; but the one thing that will help a Wellington garden to flourish is organic mulch laid on thick.

Sarah doesn't toil in her garden for hours, either; this is a deliberately easy-care garden. With a garden design business called Reviresco ('I will grow green' — her father's family motto), a busy household of adult kids who come and go and a weekend property in Otaki, time is tight. Any plant needing care and attention is not in this garden — there are no

Top row from left: Red pelargonium grown from a cutting; *Corokia* x *virgata* 'Geenty's Green'; *Abutilon* x *hybridum* 'Nabob'.
Middle row from left: *Viburnum japonicum*; black succulent *Aeonium arboreum* 'Schwarzkopf'; *Euphorbia mellifera*.
Bottom row from left: Rambling rose 'Veilchenblau'; *Teucrium fruticans*; king protea *Protea cynaroides*.

fussy annuals or perennials. A whip-around once every three weeks or so keeps the garden in trim — in two hours she can 'fix the whole blooming garden' with loppers, secateurs and a nifty tool that deals to taprooted weeds (Vita Sackville-West's favourite, apparently). She throws non-invasive weeds to the back of beds — free mulch. 'I do have quite a gung-ho approach.'

When her children were small, Sarah helped set up garden tours as a fundraiser for Wadestown school charities. She's still involved: she enjoys the people contact and well-informed feedback. And thanks to her skill, visitors to her garden find a place that never looks windblown despite the elements. It's a charming, slightly out of control, romantic country garden in town, where boundaries and fences disappear among the greenery, fulfilling Sarah's aim of creating a wondrous picture on a big canvas.

Raylene Waddell
STEWART ISLAND

IF YOU'VE NEVER BEEN TO Stewart Island, a treat awaits you: the wild beauty of this country's southernmost island settlement is a knockout. The place has a long history of people drawn to the rugged frontier; next stop, Antarctica. The weather here veers from boisterous to benign. The skies are beautiful whichever point of the compass you look towards. And while the sea is a friend one minute and a foe the next, the island is always a magnet for people who are unafraid of self-sufficiency imposed by such isolation — and for tourists drawn to the vast areas of pristine natural bush.

As for Stewart Island gardeners, call them intrepid. They scratch away on the margins of the sea and the bush. Flotsam and jetsam tempt beachcombers — especially after a storm, when seaweed is a prized harvest. In a place where animal manure is scarce, this is a peerless compost ingredient (but only after days spent soaking out the salt). Strong, salt-laden winds hammer anything above ground — animal, vegetable or mineral — though locals swear winter weather is relatively kind, and growing conditions are conducive to a wide range of tender plants. Shells come in handy for pathways, or as groundcover. Big black buoys from nearby mussel farms can be spotted everywhere, cut down into handy containers for herbs, veges and salad greens — and non edibles too.

Plants grow by trial and error. Seed and cuttings are shared among friends because, when everything arrives here by plane or ferry, new plants (and topsoil, and compost and tools) are expensive. 'But it's a rare trip to the mainland if I don't come back with boxes of plants,' says one gardener, a self-described plantaholic. 'I can't come home empty-handed.'

Previous page: The view from Raylene's upstairs balcony which takes in Iona and Ulva islands and the Paterson Inlet, shows the natural podocarp rainforest that surrounds her garden. The road arrow marks her boundary.
Top: The front garden is a magnet for curious strollers, intrigued by the native plants (astelias, hebes, grasses) with the oyster shell mulch.
Bottom: In the bush beyond the greenhouse giant tree ferns protect her edible garden from westerly winds.

Raylene Waddell, former Latin teacher, has owned Glendaruel since 1987 and has been living here permanently since her retirement in 2000. She and husband Ronnie had plans to spend their lives blissfully savouring their newfound freedom, time that had, until then, been parcelled out in school-holiday snatches. Sadly, her beloved Scotsman Ronnie died a few years into their new life . . . but Raylene takes comfort from her garden. And it's not as harsh a climate as you'd expect, she insists; to doubters, she cites the absence of hard frosts and the warming presence of an ocean current from Tasmania.

In cruise-ship season, the massive floating people-movers anchor in Paterson Inlet and send tourists ashore to the jetty at the bottom of Raylene's country lane. The curious linger by her front garden, where New Zealand native plants such as cabbage tree, flax and ponga look strange to their eyes. Here a tractor tyre is a quirky make-do Stewart Island planter; and the oyster shells that suppress weeds and keep garden paths walkable in the muddy season are a great talking point. 'We didn't eat them all,' Raylene insists. Occasionally she'll put out a pāua shell, to add a flash of iridescent blue to the mix. 'After a while it goes,' she says. 'But I don't mind if it gives people joy.'

An undistinguished, rare plant that resembles ligularia is a reminder of one of the island's oldest industries, muttonbirding. When Māori used bags made from kelp to preserve and transport their catch, they inflated the giant seaweed by blowing through the hollow stems of the megaherb *Stilbocarpa lyallii*. On a break, they made music with this natural flute. Its leaves were used to line the kelp bags, too, and when they're steamed they

Clockwise from far left: The bush is a welcoming home for birds, who provide a chirpy soundtrack to Raylene's life; rhododendrons thrive on the island and mix and mingle well with native flora; the wider leaf says this cabbage tree *Cordyline indivisa* hails from the south; extraordinary peeling bark of the tree fuchsia, *Fuchsia excorticata*.

taste rather like cabbage.

If Raylene is out front when the visitors gather, she's happy to chat. But few people get to see the best part, her main garden behind the house. The extra, unseen dimension that elevates Raylene's rear garden from cottage charmer to an emotional feast is the operatic soundtrack of birdsong. Raylene can rattle off the performers' names without even looking: tūī, kiwi, kākā, korimako, kākāriki, kererū, pīwakawaka, tomtit, shining cuckoo, blackbird, songthrush, chaffinch, starling, sparrow, red poll, seagull, black-backed gull . . . 'To see a bellbird on a yellow kniphofia is exquisite,' she says.

The birds sing all day every day. They perch in mature bush surrounding the natural amphitheatre that is her backyard, eyeing up the rich banquet of local plants and exotic lovelies, anchored by a group of mature native tree fuchsia (*Fuchsia excorticata*). The kōtukutuku, the biggest fuchsia in the world, has artistically peeling orange bark, and its nectar-rich purplish-red flowers and berries are catnip to birds. Nearby, the white flowers of a pioneer favourite hailing from Madeira, *Clethra arborea,* are another tasty treat.

Raylene's 0.1ha lot has 'very good old bones' in mature mamaku (*Cyathea medullaris*) and rhododendrons. Hers is a friendship garden: some plants that remain nameless came from cuttings brought by early pioneers, others from the gardens of friends, family and garden club stalwarts. They are no less loved than her more recent sought-out treasures, such as the towering *Allium siculum*, a honey garlic with brownish-pink flowers; or the handsome reeds of horsetail restio (*Elegia capensis*) that disguise the compost bins.

One plant that's emblematic of Raylene's

Top row from left: *Rhododendron* 'Percy Wiseman'; hebe 'Rhubarb and Custard'; an unnamed but treasured heuchera.
Middle row from left: *Stilbocarpa lyallii*; Kererū, the native woodpigeon; the mysterious mimulus.
Bottom row from left: *Eucomis comosa* 'Sparkling Dew'; *Astelia* 'Alpine Ruby'; *Fuchsia magellanica* 'Versicolor'.

horticultural tenacity is a treasured heuchera that she's kept going since 1971. It comes from her and Ronnie's first home in Gore, and it's travelled with her everywhere. 'I almost lost it once.' Cannily, she gave cuttings to friends and family, so its descendant is still with her, growing on Stewart Island.

Raylene has a thing for variegated leaves, though a visitor once told her that the received wisdom is that you can have too much. She laughs about that one. 'I think they give a softness to the garden,' she says. However, that same visitor — she calls him 'the man from the RHS' (Royal Horticultural Society) — got very excited when he spotted a rare mimulus in her border (name unknown). It's still happily thriving, secure in its anonymity.

Fruit trees are confined to espaliered crabapples, because the birds eat everything else, and a grapevine thrives snug and secure in her greenhouse. But the vege garden is a miracle of robust growth that keeps her and her guests well fed.

Raylene says in creating her garden she may have been inspired by holidays touring France, or visits to Threave Castle in Scotland. 'Yet I had no plan in mind. The garden evolved once we saw what we had.' But the way she thinks of it, she says, can best be described by the words of Elizabethan poet Robert Herrick: 'A sweet disorder in the dress . . . do more bewitch me, than when art is too precise in every part.'

Sally Allison
NORTH CANTERBURY

AN INTERNATIONAL EXPERT ON HERITAGE roses who just happens to be a Canterbury gardener, Sally Allison has spent her life growing, studying, photographing and writing about her objects of affection — and travelling widely to build her knowledge. A trip about 15 years ago to the Europa-Rosarium in Sangerhausen, Germany is still imprinted vividly on her memory. Established in 1897 to showcase new cultivars and having survived two world wars and a long spell under communism, the rosarium is now a world-class collection of roses. It was a place of delight and wonder.

And at Quarryhill Botanical Garden in Sonoma, California she revelled in a garden planted mostly from seed from Asia, where you can 'see more species of roses than you would spending weeks scouring the wilds of China'. Both destinations are standouts in a life marked by curiosity and a thirst for knowledge.

Sally has been passionate about old roses since she was a child. Her mother and grandmother were avid gardeners who took her on frequent visits to plant nurseries. In a treasured wedding photo, her mother and her four bridesmaids carry bouquets trailing great swathes of 'Cécile Brunner' roses picked from an immense bush in her grandmother's garden.

There was a time when old roses ruled. Nancy Steen inspired New Zealand gardeners almost singlehandedly with the publication of her 1966 book *The Charm of Old Roses*. She fossicked in places of early settlement, wherever missionary, farmer or goldminer lived and died, and there she rediscovered the abandoned and the obscure. Trevor Griffiths played an important role in their

Top: On a hot dry North Canterbury day, Sally heads for this lily pond, where a fringe of yellow Japanese iris and a waterspout refresh the spirits.
Bottom: A swagged rope fence (catenary) lends laidback charm to this sloping hillside, whose abundant growth is a masterful blend of roses and compatible companions.
Overleaf: Dining alfresco is a treat surrounded by scented roses and a stunning view of the Canterbury foothills across the Ashley River valley. The bronze on the farm-grown tabletop is by Virginia Marston. Front and centre is the dazzling red modern shrub rose 'Warrior'; the white rambling rose, back right, is the rare 'Thiona'; on the left, the American cultivar 'Golden Wings'; and far right, the clipped form of *Prunus* x *cistena* lends a deep red bass note to this composition. Lady's mantle and a self-seeding blue geranium soften the edges of the paving.

rehabilitation by propagating these roses for the home gardener. Sally, who had met Trevor when he was a mere apprentice, visited his heritage rose nursery in Temuka and was left spellbound. 'I knew then and there that old roses were going to be a big part of my life.'

What joy to celebrate these living antiques with enticing names such as 'Roseraie de l'Haÿ', 'Ispahan' or 'Souvenir de la Malmaison'. For about three decades, heritage roses were extremely popular. The heat may have gone off them now, but Sally has remained true to her first love. As a teenager she had already met and fallen for 'Frau Dagmar Hastrup' with its intense clove scent, satin, silver-pink flowers and golden stamens.

At Lyddington — her 4ha garden in Fernside that will be 60 this year — Sally lives and breathes old roses. But it's not a collection, she insists, 'It's a country garden full of roses' — quite probably the most comprehensive grouping of old roses in a private garden in New Zealand. A collection is a more scientific and systematic approach; Sally's choices have been less constrained.

It began in the late 1950s when Sally's mother gave her 23 roses on her twenty-third birthday. Just married, Sally was breaking in a farm garden from rough paddocks. She planted popular tea roses in an oblong bed. Delighted at the time, she shudders now at the thought of such a dull formal display.

Now, as she tootles around in her golf cart each day, visiting old favourites, checking up on stragglers, spot grooming with her secateurs, Sally revels in their names and their backstories. These climbers, ramblers, pillars, shrubs and groundcovers are real characters — they are her friends and occasionally annoying associates, rubbing shoulders in a

Right: A favourite of Sally's 'Paul's Himalayan Musk' is a vigorous David Austin rambling rose which can reach 12m. To give it a head start, she planted the rose at the same time as its sturdy supporter, a copper beech tree (*Fagus sylvatica atropurpurea*). The experiment has exceeded all expectations.

living tableau. As for their thorns: what's a few scars between friends? Then there's the unseen dimension of roses — their perfume. Wandering among Sally's roses is a sensory delight, their many scents an intense bouquet of deliciousness.

It's not all roses, of course. Sally is a consummate gardener who can grow anything with seeming ease. She loves her trees, and is especially fond of the view from the house set on a hillside looking out over the Ashley River to the foothills.

Sally's husband Bey played a crucial role as her practical and supportive right-hand man, conjuring a lake, four ponds, bridges, a mudbrick cottage, arbours and walls. 'His stamp is here everywhere with his ability to look at the bigger picture, his engineering and building skills and his affinity with diggers and bulldozers.'

This is a classic New Zealand country garden, where you meander through pockets of colour, a surprise around each corner, and where structures abound — places to stop and sit and breathe in your surroundings are everywhere, all cleverly sited so they look like they've been there forever.

Sally's bolthole up the back of the garden is an old railway carriage whose verandah drips with rambling roses. This is where she loses herself, dreams and writes. She's working on her third book, a memoir pulling together 'notes and thoughts on many aspects of my life, my family and the garden'. It will join her other titles on the bookshelf, on climbers and ramblers and on shrub roses, along with awards from local and overseas peers honouring her expert knowledge over a long and fruitful life. Sally has been a popular speaker at rose conferences over the years and

Top row from left: The upright shrub rose 'Indigo'; the rugosa rose 'Ann Endt' is named after an Auckland grower; the fragrant Bourbon rose 'Mme Lauriol de Barny'.
Middle row from left: The fragrant 'Archiduc Joseph' rose; *Rosa sericea* ssp. *omeiensis f. pteracantha* is prized for its thorns; the cold-hardy *Rosa glauca*.
Bottom row from left: The white *Rosa* x *dupontii* is a large shrub/climber; the fragrant rugosa rose 'Magnifica'; 'Frau Dagmar Hastrup'.

has rubbed shoulders with famous names in horticulture, including writers Graham Stuart Thomas, Peter Beales, Roger Phillips and Hazel Le Rougetel.

In 2015 she received the New Zealand Rose Award, and the World Rose Award in Lyon, France at the World Rose Convention, and in 2018 an Australasian rose award was added to the tally. Gardening is demanding work but, as Sally says, if you love what you are doing 'it is pure pleasure, you lose yourself in another world and count your blessings and good fortune'.

Jill Simpson
BANKS PENINSULA

FINALLY, SHE'S ADMITTED SHE NEEDS HELP. Busy gardener Jill Simpson wants an extra pair of hands to groom her hill of content, this feisty flowerbomb of a garden on the wild Pacific coast of Banks Peninsula at Fishermans Bay, where yellow-eyed penguins and fur seals cavort. Not because she's prone to sloping off or even that she's over the hill, far from it. Jill is in the mood to expand: more garden, not less, is her philosophy. Since starting in 2005, she's already created a five-star garden of national significance that unfurls across 2ha of sloping farmland; the latest project will add another five years' work to this impressive schedule.

The new zone will be even more dramatic, she promises. Just maintaining her existing garden's health and grooming all and sundry takes her three days a week. And while she likes nothing better than to spend whole days outside weeding and pruning and deadheading with just the radio for company, she keeps wanting to try new things. 'I know it's crazy.' Hence the realisation that another willing worker is essential.

What she really wants to do with the new area is to showcase native plants and exotics in striking combinations. We take the familiar for granted, yet overseas visitors covet a flax bush or consider a cabbage tree rare and unusual. In an area of paddocks 'bigger than most people's sections', Jill plans to create a distinctively different garden style with dramatic foliage. The scale of this enterprise will eat up masses of plants, mostly grown by division in her shadehouse.

This will be great news for the visitors and tourists who are being bused and choppered in by the thousands: a reason to return. They are drawn already by the singular vision

Top: Jill's passion for hebes — she has over 160 species and cultivars — is evident here in the Hebe Lawn. Clumps of white flowering *Hebe glaucophylla* thrive in high, exposed conditions and need no clipping. The low line of hebes behind is *Hebe pinguifolia* 'Sutherlandii', another cold tolerant shrub. Behind the seat is the disease-free hybrid *Hebe* 'Wiri Mist' with *Corokia* 'Frosted Chocolate'.
Bottom: In the foreground grey *Astelia nivicola* with its silver and bronze cousins lead the eye up the hill to the grey leaved Marlborough daisy with grassy spikes of aciphylla alongside.
Overleaf: White feathery fronds of the native toetoe *Cortaderia richardii* line the hillside above the easternmost point of the South Island. Beyond the unusually calm sea lies South America.

of a woman who's a painter, designer and accomplished plantswoman.

In this seaside setting at latitude 44º south, exposed to winds at times gusting to 120kph, Jill has conjured up a spellbinding garden; all the while combating rapacious rabbits and possums, which are painstakingly being phased out. As a result, the existing bush areas have sprung back to life and the farm now has at least a third of its land — 100ha — preserved as covenanted bush. Serious about conservation, Jill and husband Richard are founding members of the Banks Peninsula Conservation Trust, whose aim is to encourage locals to preserve, if not improve, biodiversity.

Over the years she's mass-planted trees for shelter, so the garden has as much wind protection as is feasible. 'It's nothing like it used to be,' she says. On the plus side, there are few frosts and the soil is rich and fertile. And unlike in the harsh conditions of the northern hemisphere, most New Zealand gardeners can potter almost all year around — we don't have to cram it all into a few months like they do, Jill points out.

The garden proper begins, logically enough, close to their old farmhouse, where food and flowers coexist. The kitchen garden is a treat for foodies. Nearby, the long border satisfies Jill's need for crowds of blooms. It's a traditional mix of roses, shrubs and perennials, she says, reflecting her personal gardening history as well as celebrating the gardens of the early French settlers in Akaroa. She gets 700–800 likes whenever she posts images of the border online; and just a fraction of that for the native plants — hence her missionary zeal to change people's hearts and minds about natives.

Clockwise from far left: Jill's perennial border shows her love of flowers and her deft artistry with colour; the productive vege garden with rustic touches has the feel of a pioneer plot; the zigzag path winds past a stream and a small spring which provide ample irrigation for this plantswoman's dream mix of penstemons, salvias, geums and grasses.

Jill is grateful to fellow lover of perennials, the Ashburton gardener Alan Trott, for gifts from an autumn garden clear-up. 'Come and see me and bring a trailer,' he told her. She vividly recalls driving down the middle of his garden while he loaded it up with treasures — some of them plants she'd never seen before — and writing up labels before she forgot their names. Among them were three or four types of persicaria, thalictrums, a really nice form of goldenrod and various phloxes. Such plants are not only hard to come by nowadays, when you *can* find them they're small and pricey. Alan's bounty came in foot-wide clumps, says Jill. 'He was doing a clear-up and being kind.' It's possible, too, that he was passing them on as insurance against their disappearance.

The zigzag garden snakes downhill beside a stream where tree ferns thrive. Against this backdrop Jill went mad with warm, bright colours and easy-care flowering plants such as daylilies, cannas, deciduous azaleas and miscanthus. Further down, subsequent planting has been influenced by the New Perennial style that's filtered across from the UK, Europe and the US, but with Jill's own twist in the selection of grasses.

Across the hill, there's a collection of 160 or so hebes, native shrubs with grand flowers. Her hankering for hebes is not something she can explain, she says, but if ever she spies a new variety she'll swoop. Jill may be a fan but she's not starry-eyed: if the plant doesn't thrive, it doesn't hang around. 'Wiri Mist', a hybrid from the series bred by Auckland Botanic Gardens manager Jack Hobbs, is a winner here at Fishermans Bay — this white flowering shrub with compact form never needs clipping. Happy hebes all, and whatever looks chirpiest, Jill propagates.

Top row from left: Speckled alstroemeria with blooms of the floribunda rose 'Eyes for You'; *Leptospermum scoparium* 'Red Damask'; *Salvia nemorosa* 'Ostfriesland'.
Middle row from left: Flowers of *Heuchera* 'Marmalade'; poppy seedlings; *Hebe* x *franciscana* 'Blue Gem'.
Bottom row from left: *Salvia* x *sylvestris* 'May Night' with geum; a scabiosa relative, *Knautia macedonica* 'Watercolours'; *Salvia* x *sylvestris* 'Blaukönigin'.

An Irish visitor commented he had never seen anything like Fishermans Bay. That pleased his hostess, who's determined to be different: 'I don't want it to be like French or Italian gardens, much as I like them.' But she does want the garden to suit its setting. In this beautiful, very dramatic place, Jill's made a garden that's a stimulating companion piece rather than a shrinking violet. 'What I've learned is that you can't go against such an amazing landscape. The garden has to work with it.'

Lyn Barnes
AUCKLAND

THIS USED TO BE A GROTTY CORNER, when Lyn Barnes bought the house opposite the graffiti-tagged motorway flyover wall. But with energy, gutsy gardening and the skills of a diplomat, she has not only beautified her own place but created a community garden next door. The once noisy, ugly area that people hurried through is now a delightful destination where you can stop to smell the flowers and marvel at the butterflies, and sometimes even buy local honey.

Eden Terrace is the remnant of an old neighbourhood sliced and diced by motorways. A small, steep pocket of characterful cottages and villas bounded by factories and offices, it's only seven minutes by electric bike to Lyn's job as a senior lecturer in journalism at Auckland University of Technology.

An early example of affordable housing, Lyn's half house was built in 1898 and never completed. When it came up for sale, she was so intrigued she ditched her modern apartment and snapped it up. She loved the idea of a small cottage with a large outdoor area: 'Apart from two swan plants out front and endless privet trees out back, it was a blank canvas.' The grass was waist-high, but she didn't care. Lyn approached Auckland Council about removing the privet and rubbish from the overgrown, unloved empty corner section next door. They helpfully obliged and she hopped over the fence to pitch in, mowing, clearing and tidying. And when a chap came to do some of her larger landscaping chores, terracing the steeper parts of her own garden, she borrowed his rotary hoe for next door and unearthed a long, narrow planting strip and two round beds.

Previous page: Approaching Lyn's corner in Eden Terrace, scaled-up butterflies and flowers in this mural by local artist Kate Millington are better than a sign. There's no mistaking the focus of this community garden.
Clockwise from top left: Old-fashioned fuchsia and roses in Lyn's front garden; the private terraces behind her house; the community garden that's tamed an unruly and unloved corner.

If the soil had been any good there she might have planted fruit trees. Instead she chose more swan plants, since they already thrived at her place. She sprinkled wildflower seeds up the strip and, apart from watering, left that garden to do its own thing while she developed the garden around her house.

After much slog, and hefting bags of compost from the zoo, Lyn's garden is now full, fragrant and flourishing. The terraced beds up the back are crammed with herbs and veges and citrus, salad greens, lemon verbena and lavender. By the studio sleepout, a wisteria-smothered pergola screens out the neighbours from above, and a trellis hides the house from below. As you sit and look through the greenery you could be forgiven for thinking there was no motorway down there and no road above. Down the side of the garden, a camellia shares a bed with vireya rhododendrons, fuchsias and hydrangeas. There are water baths everywhere for birds, bees and butterflies. Roses ramble, cleomes nod, zinnias zizz; you could be in another time zone, when women wore bustles and boots instead of trackpants and trainers.

Next door needed trees to entice more birds. Lyn asked the council, and they offered her three pūriri, whose berries are a popular avian snack food. Some kōwhai would be great too, she hinted. Yes, they had four that needed a home. 'Then I really pushed my luck by suggesting tītoki to screen the desolate area up the back.' Done. It wasn't hard getting help from the council, she explains: she had learned while setting up a farmers' market in Kerikeri that it's wise to work with rather than against bureaucracy.

It was a defining moment when Lyn realised that, despite its ugliness, the retaining

Top row from left: Tropical milkweed *Asclepias curassavica*; *Wisteria floribunda* 'Black Dragon'; Kōwhai flower *Sophora microphylla*.
Middle row from left: *Iris ensata* 'Oriental Eyes'; a puffball from a swan plant shows how it got its name; a monarch butterfly.
Bottom row from left: *Fuchsia boliviana*; Globe artichoke; *Coreopsis grandiflora* 'Sunset'.

wall opposite helped warm up the corner, encouraging butterflies to move in. The idea of a butterfly haven took off, and soon the original swan plants were joined by hundreds more. Naturally the neighbours were curious.

What with her own efforts and the sweat equity of locals, the dumping-ground-that-was has gained national recognition as the country's first urban monarch butterfly sanctuary. 'That was a great feeling,' says Lyn — not everyone gets certification from the New Zealand Moth and Butterflies Trust. Monarchs only live in a healthy environment, she says, and despite being only minutes from the city and so close to Dominion Road, this corner is insect heaven.

Lyn and neighbours formed a trust, raised money and chose mural artist Kate Millington to beautify that wall with giant kōwhai flowers and butterflies.

One side of the road was looking pretty but the other side needed help. Now there's a committee of gardeners to share the load, which frees up time for Lyn to tend her own garden. When you visit Bright Street community garden you'll see a chalkboard announcing the next working bee and workshops on composting or water collection. And you will gradually become aware of a gentle thrum of insects, not cars, and birdsong sweetening the mix. The air is full of swooping monarchs, feasting on the bright, colourful blooms and mating on the grass, and free-ranging bees darting in and out of the beehives.

How one woman can help change somewhere forlorn and sinister into a lively, warm-hearted community hub in just a few years is a remarkable story.

As Lyn says: 'I feel privileged to have found this little patch of paradise.'

Jennifer Horner
SOUTH TARANAKI

YOU DON'T EXPECT TO SEE a pile of stones in a garden of national significance, but this one at Puketarata has a special story to tell. For Jennifer Horner, the stones are a tangible link to her garden's past, when Māori worked the land. Ever since she and husband Ken bought 8ha of South Taranaki farmland in 1978, the stones keep popping up in the rich volcanic soil, and the pile keeps growing.

Jennifer, who trained as a science teacher, runs her mother's dairy farm and Ken is a lawyer in nearby Hawera. 'He works to support my gardening habit,' she says with a grin. In his spare time, Ken has delved into the history of the area and has self-published 'a vignette for those who are interested in the history of this fascinating place'. His research shows Māori lived in the area at least 400 years ago, possibly even 800 — in the nearby Keteonetea village and pā right next to the garden. The villagers grew their vegetables here in Puketarata garden, and the stones are the remains of hāngi (earth ovens).

Charmed by this backstory, Jennifer resolved to create a garden with a New Zealand feel. 'I didn't want to recreate England,' she says. But since they weren't ready to build a house or start a garden, she worked from the perimeters in, tackling steep gullies where she fattened bush remnants with native trees propagated from seeds and cuttings, as well as deciduous trees and rhododendrons. And 40 years later she's happily relishing the sight of one area that's now a covenanted stand of regenerating bush and exotics, spread over 1.7ha of river valley. At the outset Jennifer wanted to use natives as much as possible, but she has found they are not always the easiest: many of our smaller native plants do not often last long, she says.

Top: A decorative swirl of buxus hedging keeps the kitchen garden looking not just tidy but fabulous.
Bottom: Alongside the vegetable garden, the orchard is given a looser design treatment: its *Michelia yunnanensis* 'Velvet and Cream' hedge curls along the top of the slope but unlike outside, the grass inside is left to flourish.
Overleaf: A dramatic ponga palisade, reminiscent of the long-ago Māori settlement, fronted by a vibrant mix of local and exotic flora and contrasting foliage. Bold red striped canna and soldier poppies rub shoulders with Marlborough rock daisy in the foreground, while tree ferns and kauri stand to attention.

After five years of working the land — a mere blink in the life of a garden — people started to take notice. Jennifer's 'Dynamic Landscape Garden' was featured in a 1990 Japanese book, *Woman's Garden*. Nowadays visitors to Puketarata will find a mature garden with an exciting range of native and exotic planting spread over 0.6ha that's wholly sympathetic to the wider landscape. Lavish rhododendron and azalea displays in spring beckon busloads of gardeners during the annual Taranaki Garden Festival. The grounds are peppered with contemporary outdoor sculptures, and a stunning palisade entrance built of ponga (tree fern *Cyathea dealbata*) logs leads to the kitchen gardens, where there is a decorative buxus parterre, and herb and vege gardens that bulge with produce.

As you wander through, you'll find some rare treasures. Near the front door to the house, a tree that resembles a walking stick sprouting mini pineapples is Jennifer's favourite New Zealand native plant: so singular and striking is *Dracophyllum traversii* that it could be her garden's emblem. This plant is notoriously hard to propagate: if you see one in the wild, take a photo instead of taking it home; and if you see one at a garden centre or specialist nursery, swoop. But the odds are against that. Draped over the house pergola is the once rare climbing *Tecomanthe speciosa* — it has lush green leaves with fragrant, waxy cream flowers that only reveal themselves to people looking out from inside the house. A living sculpture consisting of a group of three mature cabbage trees (*Cordyline australis*) act as guardians or kaitiaki near the gap in the ponga palisade.

Views are key to the way Jennifer's garden developed. 'The inland view northeast is what

Top row from left: Feathery leaves of the native rimu *Dacrydium cupressinum*; the distinctive silvery form of the Marlborough rock daisy; this Ilam azalea was named after Jennifer's grandmother 'Louisa Williams'. **Middle row from left:** 'Mi Amor' rhododendron cannot be beaten for winter fragrance; the decorative *Allium hollandicum* 'Purple Sensation'; *Aloe plicatilis*. **Bottom row from left:** *Cordyline* 'Red Fountain' grows in a clump; *Dracophyllum traversii*; *Astelia chathamica* 'Silver Spear'.

OVERLEAF

Clockwise from top left: On the top terrace azaleas and rhododendrons, including the yellow/orange 'C.I.S', line up under a row of cabbage trees; view across the covenanted bush Jennifer planted all those years ago; Mt Taranaki, a constant presence, and venue for skiing excursions when the garden is asleep for winter; hāngi rocks, unearthed frequently as Jennifer cultivates her garden, are a link to an earlier time.

sold us on the property,' she says. And quite often you can see Mt Taranaki, which she's skied down twice, she says matter of factly. And then there are the many ancient pā sites on surrounding hilltops to contemplate.

Their low-profile house was dug into the hillside to preserve these important sightlines and gain shelter from the persistent westerly and cool southerly winds. A large lawn at the front and a tennis court lower down set the scene. As Jennifer's garden grew, it radiated from the house in long terraces, using an invisible ha-ha instead of an intrusive fence to mark the northern boundary.

The view from the house to the garden was just as important to her planting schemes. Jennifer devised a technique of placing shrubs and plants just so, then dashing back to the house to check how they looked from the inside. After all, she says, that's the main vantage point. We spend most of our lives inside looking out, she explains. Only when she got their placement right would she dig them in. And after decades of growth the house has settled into the garden, becoming an integral part of its design.

What with all the native plants and an active predator-trapping programme (rat and possum cafés, Jennifer calls them), Puketarata now trills to the sounds of happy native birds. They in turn make their own contributions, which, in due course, grow into more native plants. Grateful though Jennifer is, sometimes it's too much of a good thing: that's when she kits up in waterproof overtrousers and raincoat for a muddy crawl through the undergrowth to thin out and weed. A happy gardener.

Sal Gordon
AUCKLAND

GOOSEBUMPS ALERT: ON A HOT SPRING afternoon in Sal Gordon's Freemans Bay garden, full to bursting with foliage of every colour, shape and form, it's getting rowdy and emotional. We're in the afternoon-tea segment of the day rather than cocktail time, so this is no happy-hour hysteria. It's *something* though. Sal's subtropical succulent backyard is otherworldly and exotic. Vibrant. Sensual. Exciting. These are words that pop into your head as you slowly take stock of your surroundings. The front garden is equally full of dramatic delights.

If your gardening experience is defined by perennial borders and roses rambling over a pergola, Sal's place might come as a shock. Even if you think you know about succulents because you've got a couple of potted aloes, this is a master class in using them.

'The only thing I would have done differently,' says Sal, 'is to have done all this 20 years ago. I've wasted years mindlessly weeding.' Weeding is what got her into this in the first place: she was sick to death of it. Before, she had a lot of the same plants and a vege garden up the back, 'but design-wise it was a bit of a dog's breakfast'. It needed a revamp.

At the time her partner John Green was sailing around the world and she thought she'd like her bit of pleasure on the home front. For advice, she turned to her close buddy, garden designer Trish Bartleet. 'I'm a messy person. I needed her to tidy me up.' They'd met years before when their kids were little and they were both studying landscape design. Sal was a physiotherapist by training, but she wanted a change of direction. Juggling part-time work with lectures, she graduated and went to work with Trish, doing some of her own projects,

Previous page: It's a most unusual front garden for a villa. Instead of traditional lawns and rosebeds, you'll see Canary Island dragon trees (*Dracaena draco*) with New Zealand cabbage trees, fat green heads of *Ligularia reniformis*, and black and green succulent rosettes, fringed with coral-flowered *Russelia equisetiformis*.
Top: View from the front verandah towards the downtown Sky Tower.
Bottom: Out front, looking up to the vege garden, another break from suburban gardening custom of spuds and cabbages being hidden away at the back.

too. After a few years she stowed away the gumboots and headed back to the physio clinic to generate regular income. But her spell of working in the gardening world was a blast that really opened her eyes, though she never felt confident as a designer: 'I'm probably better at the plant side of things.'

In answer to her SOS call, Trish came back with a much bigger scheme than Sal expected. She's never regretted it. In the front garden, where the Sky Tower and skyscrapers dominate the skyline, haphazardly arranged citrus trees were shifted aside and a wheelbarrow waltz began. Now, as you approach the gate, you're greeted by cabbage trees, flax and *Dracaena draco*. Along the front boundary, a hedge of the orange firecracker plant *Russelia equisetiformis* tumbles over the fence. Up the front steps the traditional villa front garden is nowhere to be seen: instead of being hidden down the back, vegetable beds thrive here in a display that's as tactile as it is bright and colourful all year round.

A line-up of ponytail palms (*Beaucarnea recurvata*) swish their strappy, curly leaves above beds of glossy green and black *Aeonium arboreum* and ice-blue *Senecio serpens*. The large, shiny leaves of *Ligularia reniformis* are a shapely addition to this crowd.

Around the back, past a *Muehlenbeckia complexa* privacy screen for the downstairs flat on one side and fragrant brugmansia further up, Trish has worked more miracles. The deck that opens off a contemporary kitchen/living room had always been too small. 'Trish made us change it,' says Sal. Now it's much more in scale with a lawn that's surrounded by beds of sizzling succulents, bromeliads and cycads. Next to a dining-out spot, a small water feature with goldfish contributes the sound of

Clockwise from top left: Silverbeet and lettuce grow in raised beds surrounded by dramatic foliage; Gretchen Albrecht's sculpture Threshold-Shift; Sal grows mostly her own cuttings to fatten up succulents beds; the Vietnamese bowl anchors a group of strappy-leaved echium, canna and bromeliads.

trickling water. From here you look down to a focal point of gnarly feijoa trees, shading a smaller table setting with peacock chairs.

On the higher side, to the left of the kitchen, there's a hedge like no other: a lineup of *Doryanthes palmeri*. Hailing from Australia, the giant spear lily looks like it's been raised on steroids — yet it's tough and hardy. Tall *Aloe bainesii* share privacy duties up by the back boundary.

Tumbling down to the back lawn is a sequence of tactile, colour-saturated leaf forms: purple *Strobilanthes gossypinus*, yellow and stripy-orange canna, hot pink *Iresine herbstii*, green cycads and silver agave. Across the lawn are straight-trunked nīkau, underplanted with purple-tipped *Liriope muscari* and bromeliads in every shade of green, grey and red. The burgundy leaves of *Cercis canadensis* 'Forest Pansy' flutter above.

The lawn keeps all this bright magnificence grounded. Boundaries dissolve, hidden by a mass of red and green foliage. The more you look, the more mesmerising it becomes, and that's when the goosebumps appear . . . which is where we came in.

Sal says choosing the right plant for the site is the best advice she ever got, probably from Trish. Plants have got to be bulletproof. Gone are the days when she would loiter in a garden centre for inspiration: mostly she propagates her own plants from cuttings.

And she studies the work of people she admires. The Brazilian landscape designer Roberto Burle Marx was a particular hero. 'Trish and I were all set to go to Brazil and he up and died. Made Wijaya in Bali was another inspiration. He died too. I'm not naming any more designers.' A visit to the late opera singer Ganna Walska's Lotusland garden in

Left: A mind-boggling mix of leaf shape and colour adds up to low-maintenance care — provided you don't mind mosquito bites and cuts from sharp edged bromeliads.

OVERLEAF

Top row from left: *Russelia equisetiformis*; a two-toned sport of ornamental taro; *Neoregelia* 'Pink Champagne'.
Middle row from left: *Strobilanthes dyerianus* aka Persian shield; the succulent *Senecio serpens*; the matchstick bromeliad from southern Brazil, *Aechmea gamosepala*.
Bottom row from left: The Northland-bred bromeliad *Neoregelia* 'Kahala Dawn'; *Vriesea* 'Kiwi Sunset'; a bromeliad flower poking through the fleshy leaves of an aloe.
Facing page: A stately cycad with fringed leaves, a giant taro and its finer leaved cousin are warmed up by the purple-veined Persian shield.

California had a lasting impact: it's eccentric, quirky and amazing, says Sal.

The only way to visit Sal's garden, which is private, is if she pitches in and opens her gate to fundraising tours. And in the meantime, she's working out how to create a wall of tiny tillandsia along the back fence.

Margaret Barker
DUNEDIN

THE GARDEN AT LARNACH CASTLE IS pushing 150 years old yet it's looking more distinguished than dated, thanks to its devoted owner of the past 50 years, Margaret Barker. Tourists flock to the castle and garden, and locals choose its dramatic setting on the Otago Peninsula as a backdrop for their rites of passage or a jolly good knees-up. As for garden lovers, they'll find here an all-seasons feast of diversity, a superb synthesis of Victorian and contemporary ideas, native and exotic plants — and, thanks to its temperate coastal climate, it's all in rude good health.

With great panache and years of demanding work, Margaret's castle garden is brighter and better looking than its founder — Australian banker, merchant and politician William Larnach — could have envisaged when he built his dream home here in the 1870s. The goldrush helped Larnach become a wealthy man in boomtown Dunedin and after finding the right piece of land, 14ha of rolling hills with a panoramic view of the town and harbour, he lavished a fortune on creating a suitably grand Gothic Revival-style castle made of stone. He planted shelterbelts of exotic and native trees, built a fashionable glasshouse for his fern collection, and erected rose tunnels underplanted with his favourite foxgloves. A farm garden and orchard supplied produce to feed visitors and family.

But after Larnach took his own life in 1898, the castle and its estate fell into disrepair. It sprang back to life in the 1930s when the Purdie family turned it into a popular visitor attraction, but after they sold it, the place languished again.

Fast forward to 1967 when curious young holidaymakers Margaret and Barry Barker drove up. They found a ruined castle, more

Left: The garden around the front of Larnach Castle shows Margaret's clever mix of ancient and modern, local and introduced. An Irish yew tree echoes the shape of the castle's tower, whose entrance is flanked by local cabbage trees (*Cordyline australis*). In the Patterned Garden, a buxus hedge outlines an azalea bed, with colourful Scottish heathers to the left, while purple *Thalictrum delavayi* 'Hewitt's Double' tower above it all.
Overleaf: The glorious golden arch of *Laburnum x watereri* 'Vossii', pictured in late spring with spent spring bulbs at their feet, is a favourite spot for wedding photographs. Cleverly framing the soft shape of Saddle Hill to the south, the pergola ends in a reflecting pool with marble sculpture 'Spiritual Waka' by Ray Ansin.

gothic horror than palatial estate, in dire need of life support. Everywhere they looked, the property was crying out for not just a revival but for a heart transplant. A money pit, of course, but wouldn't it be lovely, they thought . . . And, just like in a fairy tale, the Barkers bought a castle. Barry was interested in getting into the tourist industry and saw its potential as a visitor attraction. Margaret was fascinated by its history, the buildings, the stone walls and the ambience.

It was a huge challenge, but Margaret eventually transformed the grounds into an enchanting, dreamy, six-star garden of international significance. At last count it welcomes about 100,000 visitors a year. Tourists rock up from all over the world to be welcomed by Margaret's team of up to 90 tartan-liveried staff. On one day in the cruise-ship season, 19 coachloads of visitors arrived for the full Larnach Castle experience. That calls for a slick organisation. They may never meet head gardener and native plant expert Fiona Eadie, but her team's work speaks for itself.

For Margaret, the garden is her pride and joy — and it all began with a puzzle. 'Where is the rock garden?' demanded an elderly visitor with a long memory. Margaret didn't even know she had a rock garden but eventually it was found buried under a mound of scrub. 'Clearing the lost rock garden from the 1930s was a no-brainer,' she says. And as she hacked through the jungle of blackberry, berberis, sycamore and macrocarpa, and sourced plants to suit this world in miniature, she developed a taste for alpines and a thirst for botanical information. Nowadays she shares her encyclopaedic plant knowledge with readers of *NZ Gardener* magazine.

Top left: Margaret originally designed the Serpentine Walk as a January showcase but gradually this double border has evolved to extend the flowering season. Seen here are the pink *Silene viscosa*, yellow *Anthemis tinctoria* 'E. C. Buxton' and purple *Geranium x magnificum*.
Top right: Beyond the rhododendrons is the second most photographed feature (after the ducks), the Alice in Wonderland-inspired red heart chair, with 'Stead's Best' rhododendron in the foreground.
Bottom: This spectacular view taken from the South Seas Garden sweeps up the Otago Harbour to its mouth. There it meets the Pacific Ocean whose islands inspired Margaret's dream of hunting down this unique plant collection.

OVERLEAF
Top left: In early spring, Margaret's passion for snowdrops is evident with *Galanthus nivalis* growing below the dogwoods, *Cornus controversa*.
Bottom left: The same scene later in spring, one misty morning.
Top right: The stately arches of macrocarpa took 10 years to form. In The Field the Irish snowdrop *Galanthus* 'Straffan' encircles the base of an English beech tree.
Bottom right: Standing out against this misty backdrop, a pair of Irish yews is reflected in the pond.

Over the years plants have lured Margaret around the world, hunting them down to their native habitats to see for herself what makes them tick, rather than relying on book learning. And her travels are not for the faint-hearted; she's a tramper and a trekker rather than a pampered tourist, camping in the Andes, climbing Mt Gower on Lord Howe Island, bunking down on a Russian polar vessel, finding crown imperials (fritillarias) in the mountains of Iran.

As the mother of two babies (Sophie and Norcombe), Margaret found the rock garden was a manageable project that could be fitted in while she renovated the castle interior. With the help of her mother she completed the rockery in stages, and this gave her plenty of thinking time before she attacked the rest of the garden. Margaret says each new garden project evolved in her mind's eye long before it was developed on the ground. 'I have a creative engine inside of me that keeps on going,' she says. Working with nature, seeing how the garden changes as plants go through their seasonal cycles, is personally rewarding, she says; and the physical work calms her. 'The garden is my happy place.'

Rockeries are not to everyone's taste, but it's part of Larnach's backstory that she is keen to honour. Besides, Margaret has not madly followed the latest trends if she doesn't like them. Her flower-crammed perennial border, the Serpentine Walk — named for its meandering path — was installed in the mid-1970s and was designed 'to evoke the country garden era before the First World War', because she likes that style. Since then it's had mere tweaks rather than makeovers.

Not for her the herd-like rush to instal posh potagers, modernist metallics or pebbled

Top row from left: The Himalayan blue poppy *Meconopsis* 'Lingholm'; *Celmisia semicordata*; the white climbing Chilean bellflower, *Lapageria rosea* var. *albiflora*.
Middle row from left: *Agave palmeri* from the American Southwest, thriving in the South Seas Garden; Alice by Stephen Gleeson on the Wishing Well Lawn; Kaka beak *Clianthus puniceus* var *maxius*.
Bottom row from left: The giant snowdrop *Galanthus elwesii* 'Emerald Hughes'; *Chionochloa rubra*; blue *Rhododendron augustini* ssp. *chasmanthum*.

minimalism. But she has had fun with one 'hot' trend from the 1860s, inspired by Lewis Carroll's bestseller *Alice's Adventures in Wonderland*. People from all over the world are familiar with Alice and the Cheshire Cat and other characters from the book's fantasy world, and they love to be photographed sitting on the giant red-hearted throne beside the temperate rainforest.

Come November the golden laburnum-draped pergola frames a breathtaking view of Saddle Hill to the south. Blue rhododendrons and a native plantation beckon the curious. The South Seas Garden features plants from around the Pacific and, from its belvedere, you can glimpse the ocean beyond the harbour mouth. This section is a marvel of colour and succulents with a palmy, tropical feel — and yet here they all are, thriving in the snowbelt.

Margaret says she still gets a thrill when people choose the castle garden to celebrate milestones in their lives. 'And the nicest thing anyone said to me? That this garden lifted their spirits.'

The charm of Larnach lies in the way the garden enhances and softens the castle's stonework, while celebrating views of the sky, city and harbour. And on quiet misty days, when the light is pearly, the whole place is mysteriously veiled. Sounds are muffled, except for plops of moisture dripping from trees. That's when you get a sense of what this land was like when William Larnach first arrived. And as the mist clears and the castle comes into view, you could be forgiven for mistaking this place for a setting from a fairy tale.

Rose Thodey
AUCKLAND

SIZE ISN'T EVERYTHING. Nor is the girth of your wallet. And as for following the latest shiny trend, forget about it. For a garden to thrill it must have atmosphere, something intangible but unforgettable. Rose Thodey believes atmosphere is the quality that defines a successful garden — and she should know. Not only is her small, chic Auckland city garden the epitome of elegance, it has atmosphere in spades.

Rose has written about gardens for years for newspapers and magazines and she's the author of several influential books on old roses and garden design. As well as being a knowledgeable plantswoman, she's a design enthusiast and a member of the Garden Design Society of New Zealand. Part of her remit has been to organise a tour of Auckland gardens every two years, to promote the work of local designers and raise money for charity. It doesn't automatically follow that someone who loves design will have a beautiful garden at home; but Rose loves nothing better than to mess about in her own plot — which other people swoon over if they are lucky enough to visit.

This farmer's daughter from Taihape grew up learning about planting at her mother's knee. She says her earliest memories are of wandering 'free as I pleased' around their rambling, English-inspired country garden with round lawn and old-fashioned flowers that she was encouraged to pick. Her mother was a born gardener and couldn't help herself, she says.

When Rose and husband Chris moved north to Auckland from Wellington in 1986 they were looking for a house with a family-friendly garden that she could tame while raising two children — soon to number four. In those days

Top: A neighbourly approach to narrow entrances where fences make way for a shared path and upright copper beech tree.
Bottom: Down by the pergola you could be forgiven for thinking the city was miles away.
Overleaf: The curves of the borrowed landscape (Rangitoto Island in the Hauraki Gulf) are reflected in the design elements of this small urban garden, where the Sky Tower lines up nicely with Rose's rill.

Freemans Bay was an underappreciated — and hence affordable — area just five minutes from Queen Street. Its old wooden villas had a familiar vibe to someone coming from Wellington. This feels like us, they said to each other, even before seeing the million-dollar views of the harbour and the skyscrapers downtown.

On this small section (582m^2) with a solid clay base, she uncovered some plant treasures that had survived in pockets of rich dark loam. Tucked below the Ponsonby ridge, the garden feels extremely sheltered and warm — apart from when it's hit by the occasional northerly. Initially Rose boxed on with the sloping lawn, clearing away weeds and poorly placed trees and shrubs. But once they decided to create a full-height basement with bedrooms for the teenagers, a garden revamp became a real and exciting possibility.

Conservation architect Graeme Burgess took care of the house renovation while his wife and fellow architect Lucy Treep created a new landscape design. 'The oval lawn was a masterstroke and endlessly pleasing,' says Rose. And thanks to Lucy's clear-sighted layout she could enjoy herself planting within the boundaries of hard landscaping — Tuscan sandstone and capped brick walls you can perch on. 'That was another of Lucy's lightbulb moments.'

Serenity is a word that comes to mind when contemplating the results 30 years on. Colours are soft and gentle, with her favourite blue setting the tone. The plant selection is connoisseur level. You don't often see the scented, soft apricot noisette rose 'William Allen Richardson' (1878) that's growing here on the boundary fence. Nor 'Souvenir de St Anne's', a Bourbon rose whose almost

Top row from left: *Rosa* 'Eglantyne'; *Pittosporum cornifolium* from the Poor Knights Islands; star jasmine, the scented *Trachelospermum jasminoides*. **Middle row from left:** The upright copper beech *Fagus sylvatica* 'Dawyck Purple'; the Lord Howe wedding lily *Dietes robinsoniana*; *Salvia* 'Wendy's Wish' popping through a bed of *Orlaya grandiflora*. **Bottom row from left:** *Lobelia siphilitica* aka the great blue lobelia; *Myrsine divaricata* 'Poor Knights'; *Hydrangea macrophylla* 'Trophy'.

single, palest blush-pink flowers are intensely fragrant and bloom continuously. And, to its great credit, this sport or mutation of 'Souvenir de la Malmaison' does not turn to mush in the rain. To the right of the birdbath is another curiosity, *Neomarica caerulea*, which resembles an iris but is a subtropical. Rose is mad about *Myrsine divaricata* 'Poor Knights': she's got a couple of these slow-growing weeping matipo in pots by the front door, and around by the ryegrass lawn she's used a row of them in a clipped buxus-style hedge. Its charming heart-shaped leaves subtly echo the heart motif in a chimney pot rescued from above the original kitchen.

The climbing frame in the potager was inspired by a visit to the Getty Museum garden in Los Angeles. The glass birdbath and fish in the water feature are by Jenny McLeod. A later addition is the pool off the family room, which was designed by Gudrun Fischer. And on the fence above there's another water feature with a nīkau sculpture by Roderick Burgess.

Rose's garden must work at every level. From the verandah on the middle floor of the house, it's hard to tear your eyes away from the view of Rangitoto Island. But look below and the shape of the elliptical lawn and the pleasing symmetry of the groundworks become apparent. Down there, walking among the plants, it's an enclosed private world full of scent and other sensory delights.

'Gardening to me is a bit like an addiction that you have to indulge on a fairly regular basis,' says Rose. 'Luckily I'm an optimist and most things thrive. I find weeding therapeutic but don't know when to stop. Over the years I've learned to mix up gardening tasks — that helps with the wear and tear on the body.' She's also patient: 'The results when a new

Left: A nīkau bronze by Roderick Burgess is an elegant addition poolside.

plant bursts into flower overnight, or when a grouping finally looks exactly right after much trial and error, is my reward.'

She loves her creative hobby. 'You're using living, growing, changing materials, and that makes it challenging and fascinating. Because the results are never predictable. There is nothing more satisfying than a few hours' grooming and weeding — what my mother called "a good clearance". It makes a glass of wine on a summer's evening feel well deserved.'

Liz Morrow
MATAKANA

YOU GO TO OMAIO TO SEE THE GARDEN and you stay for what's unseen. At Liz Morrow's exciting coastal property on the Takatu Peninsula, an hour north of Auckland city, there's an indefinable feeling. Omaio gets under your skin — living up to its name as a place of peace, quiet and tranquillity.

Visitors have different and often surprising emotional reactions, says Liz. Some are moved to tears. Perhaps it's the whispering breezes ruffling the leaves. Maybe it's all that bracing sea air acting as a tonic. Or the sense of calm as you walk through a cathedral-like grove of ancient pūriri, tōtara, kōwhai and kauri, accompanied by live birdsong in place of plainsong. Church was never like this. You linger a bit longer, stroll through the bush again, admire the koru-shaped vege garden at the end of Jane's Lane, and follow the trail down through another grove of mature native trees to Johny's Deck, a wooden platform perched above the waves.

As you wind your way back to the log cabin where Liz lives surrounded by paintings of flowers, you become acutely aware of the way she has subtly shaped the curved garden beds to echo the contours of the land. The bush dictated what could grow in its shade; the trees demanded respect, and what Liz has planted not only feels right, everything is growing harmoniously.

The Morrows bought this 7ha property in 1980 and for years used it as a family holiday bach. With great foresight Liz vowed to protect the sickly bush from predators: on day one of taking ownership, in went a fence to keep out cattle and sheep, and a programme of pest control began. 'Hundreds of possums were trapped in those early days,' she says. It's down to two a year now. But she still has bait

Clockwise from top left: The entrance to Omaio is a triumph of handcrafted naturalism, with native tree ferns and bird sculptures by Rebecca Rose standing by to greet visitors; detail of Liz's raised vege bed built in the shape of a koru; repeat planting makes for a relaxed setting where Jane's Lane leads to the kitchen (koru) garden.
Overleaf: In spring the native bush gets a blast of colour when massed clivia begin their long blooming season.

stations and traps to deter rats, mice, stoats, weasels and possums. And thanks to the combined efforts of Liz and her neighbours, the birds are back and there's even talk of the kiwi returning.

Liz wasn't even tempted to start a garden back then. At home in St Heliers, Auckland, she lived a full life raising son Johny and daughter Jane, while creating a notable and popular English-style garden that was open to visitors almost from the beginning. A demon for work, she was into everything horticultural: from clubs to charity fundraisers. She was also involved at the beginning of the Ellerslie Flower Show as exhibition manager, and she opened her garden to raise money for the Anglican Holy Trinity Cathedral. Roles in the Royal New Zealand Institute of Horticulture, along with managing Eden Garden in Epsom for 10 years, kept her fully engaged.

Then, in 2005, her focus changed: she decided to sell up in Auckland and move permanently to the cabin on the coast, where she would establish a garden. 'I was 58 and wanted to achieve it by the time I was 60. Rather an ambitious plan.'

Though she describes herself as a bull at a gate, the Omaio project was at first a study in patience. She walked around for at least six months, making shapes on the lawn with garden hoses, until she was ready to start digging new beds. She had hundreds of roses in her city garden, but they wouldn't do in this native bush setting; nor would her other favourites — camellias and azaleas. 'It was important that I didn't use plant material that clashed or argued with my surroundings. I needed to find plants that married well and held hands with what existed.'

Below the beautifully regenerating native

Top row from left: *Hydrangea arborescens* 'Annabelle'; pale lemon clivia; the native fern *Blechnum novae-zelandiae*.
Middle row from left: Nīkau frond; *Rudbeckia fulgida* 'Goldsturm'; *Coprosma repens* 'Poor Knights'.
Bottom row from left: *Ligularia dentata* 'Britt-Marie Crawford'; *Bergenia cordifolia* 'Beethoven'; the silver fern *Cyathea dealbata*.
OVERLEAF
Top left: Few gardens can boast native trees of such antiquity yet Liz is the proud caretaker of ancient kauri trees with one that's 1000 years old.
Top right: To be able to visit a puriri that's 1500 years old is a rare treat.
Bottom left: Courtside artistry in the form of teak and iron tennis balls (the latter by Jeff Thomson) seemingly spilling away from the tennis court, show Liz's sense of fun.
Bottom right: A view from the lower deck named for Liz's son Johny who aims for Kawau Island when hitting golf balls.

shrubs and trees, including a 1500-year-old pūriri, she's introduced shade-loving clivias by the thousands, bergenias, hydrangeas, ferns, hostas and rengarenga lilies. Mostly, but not exclusively native shrubs, the garden's a fusion of plants that suit the setting. And when fat birds drop seeds indiscriminately, she just shrugs her shoulders and concedes squatters' rights to the seedlings that sprout.

Closer to the cabin she's had fun with secateurs, clipping native shrubs into soft forms and fat rounds, and there's a changing display of potted colour in tune with the seasons. Relaxed and easy on the eye is the effect she was aiming for, with tones of green the dominant colour note. She's blurred the sharp line of the tennis-court fence, with larger-than-life shrubs cut into the shape of tennis balls; these join ball sculptures dotted across the lawn that roll into the shrubbery.

A permanent helping hand would have been useful in the earlier days, but having been raised in the King Country in a DIY family, Liz says, she managed very well alone. But she credits Johny and Jane for their practical and motivational help, and local man Lance Michell comes every week to manage lawns, bush trails and driveway. Even with the main garden tasks completed, Liz is always busy. Besides weeding and grooming outdoors every day, she runs a B&B, and plays bridge and mah-jong.

All this arduous work outdoors has its rewards. Omaio, like all New Zealand Gardens Trust gardens, is assessed every three years to ensure standards are maintained, and in April 2017 Liz got an upgrade to the highest category: with six stars, Omaio is now a garden of international significance.

Lyn Eglinton
WAIRARAPA

THE ENTRANCE TO LYN EGLINTON'S property near Masterton is only a small taste of what's to come. An elegant grouping of four black posts either side of the cattle stop can be taken at face value. But venture further into Denfield and you enter a place that's a sampler of the history of garden design, featuring a dazzling cast of characters — André Le Nôtre, Vita Sackville-West, Russell Page, Fernando Caruncho, the Wirtz family. Each has played a part in inspiring Lyn's contemporary twist on the classic garden.

But this garden designer had other ideas when she scribbled the first drawing. 'I wanted it to be an entrance that's definite, though not like a gated village or retirement home. I was going for something simple and country, and definitely not pretentious.' She wanted to suggest the tall chimney tops of the board-and-batten house beyond, and because they mark the beginning of a long driveway, it seemed to her she needed two indicators — hence the double pillars. She hoped it would be New Zealand enough. Maybe the little steel caps came from the need to sluice away rain, or maybe there's a whiff of a Medici cap from a Renaissance painting.

A word about the driveway: an existing farm track already lined with poplars, it's been beefed up with a second row of these trees. Lyn was thinking of the country roads and canal paths in France that Napoleon steepled with trees to provide deep shade for his army. She would have preferred linden trees or chestnuts, 'but I wanted to be able to see them mature before I die!' Lyn loves the way these 'heaven trees' as she calls them, link blue sky to green hills, especially in the Wairarapa, with its wide panoramas.

At the end of the drive a second entrance

Top: Sentry boxes, sculpture, gate posts, or all three. The entrance to Lyn's garden promises something special at the end of the drive that's lined with double rows of trees inspired by Napoleon.
Bottom: A grid of pleached hornbeam *Carpinus betulus* 'Fastigiata' to the left of the entrance courtyard. Lyn loves their shadow play.
Overleaf: This gardener loves green and buxus and giving nature a nudge. Yet Lyn reckons it takes next to no time to keep her topiary in shape and, cannily, she plants lady's mantle *Alchemilla mollis* at their feet to discourage weeds.

punctuates a solid wall — built because she didn't want vehicles to approach the house without pausing, she explains. Walls are hugely important in traditional Persian gardens, a design style that's never dated. And Lyn has always loved 'those funny little doors in a wall in Spain or Morocco' that promise as much as they hide.

Lyn sees her garden as a living three-dimensional sculpture. 'Aspects change daily but static elements do not,' she explains. 'Weather, time of day, light and shadow reflect the mood and talk back to us. Drama and theatre abound. A careful walled approach delivers an installation waxing and waning but forever calm and dependable in a frantic world.'

Once inside the courtyard, the weary visitor is immediately cheered by the sight of a sparkling oblong pond. Water is a welcoming gesture of hospitality, in the Persian manner. But it's also a mirror reflecting house and garden and sky. All this before you get to see what's growing in the garden.

Lyn and husband Hop built the house in 2008 before starting on the garden. It's a contemporary Georgian-style home with a New Zealand twist and they painted it black. Lying slightly east of north, it captures sun all day, thanks to Lyn's non-negotiable demand for high doors and low-sashed windows.

'An aspiring garden-maker requires a man as her major asset,' she says, paying homage to Hop. 'He will require patience, humour and basic kitchen skills and agree to all things gardening. Rid yourself of the type who holds opinions on anything horticultural, particularly design. Seek out the rare all-rounder who will dig those holes and distribute compost while stringing out the best

Clockwise from top left: Frugal the Scottish terrier obviously belongs in this green and black wonderland; the path leading to the chimney is lined with pleached rows of *Tilia cordata*, the small-leaved linden tree; black mondo grass *Ophiopogon planiscapus* points the way to the farmland beyond.

string line, because he respects your wishes. Once found he will agree that sitting down is not an option.' Lucky Lyn.

Her garden began in a large paddock within a 16ha block, half at one level, then falling away to a terrace of much the same size. In designing gardens, Lyn says she's always aiming for light and shadow effects. Nowadays she gets a real thrill seeing (through her tall windows) the way the sun moves around her garden.

To describe it as low-maintenance would be to damn it with faint praise (let's not, though it is surprisingly easy to look after). Think of it instead as a structured garden along classical lines, where hedges tall (hornbeam, beech) and short (buxus of every variety) contain a private world enlivened by a million shades of green. Created within shelterbelts of poplar and *Cupressus leylandii* (close-planted so these quick-growing cypresses stretch up rather than sprawl), the garden rooms around the house are places of serenity and calm.

Their settled air belies their youth: Lyn always has buxus plants on the go in a shadehouse — she doesn't have the patience to put in little cuttings, she explains. She popped trees and shrubs into seemingly bottomless and highly nutritious river-silt loam, applied water (having a bore water supply is an advantage) and stood back. An occasional handful of blood and bone, thick layers of homemade compost and bark mulch to protect against drying winds in October and November, and a clip once a year is all the caretaking her garden needs. Within the hedged garden beds, Lyn grows peonies, heritage roses and at least 300 white or cream hydrangeas — 'Annabelle', 'Snowball',

Top: In the quince avenue where a foaming understorey of oak-leaved *Hydrangea quercifolia* is turning red in early autumn.
Bottom: How many ways can you play with trees? Lyn thinks nothing of limbing up, pleaching, hedging, tweaking and taming.

'Limelight', 'Kyushu' and 'Fuji Waterfall', to name a few. Clipping and cloud-pruning bay, buxus, hornbeam (*Carpinus betulus*) and *Juniperus chinensis* 'Kaizuka' conifers — in fact anything that's soft and pliable — is her idea of fun.

Lyn credits the wisdom of role models, including the late Russell Page; whenever she's stuck, she goes back to the English celebrity designer's only book, *The Education of a Gardener*, written in 1962. Then there's the father of her favourite French style, Le Nôtre, the celebrated gardener to King Louis XIV, whose masterpiece is Versailles. Present-day inspiration comes from the Spanish minimalist Fernando Caruncho, and the Wirtz family — contemporary Belgian designers who have elevated hedges to a higher plane.

And first and foremost, she'll never forget a moment when, as a young woman, she sat still in Vita Sackville-West's deserted study overlooking the garden at Sissinghurst. 'It made me aware of excellence in design and the importance of the discerning eye.' Back then, long before this garden became world famous, it was all slightly shabby. 'But the magic has never left me. How lucky I was.'

Penny Zino
NORTH CANTERBURY

YOU MIGHT THINK THAT AFTER WORKING in a garden you started from scratch over 50 years ago you had earned some down time, a chance to smell the old-fashioned roses perhaps, or to soak up the alpine views. But Penny Zino, owner of Flaxmere Garden in Hawarden, in the northwest foothills of the Canterbury rural heartland, is always on the go. She's usually out of bed at 6.30am for an energising cold swim, which sets her up for a day's work in her 3.2ha garden. It's a full day. She doesn't down tools and park the barrow until late, when lack of daylight drives her inside to cook dinner. 'Nowadays I do stop at lunchtime,' she says. 'I've learned to listen to my body.'

Penny says she always feels most at peace in the garden she started in 1966 as husband John's new bride, 'and that's probably what keeps me going. I love the feeling of physical tiredness after a long day outside.' She also learned to live with very little sleep — if she can get five or six hours' shuteye, that'll do. It wouldn't suit everyone, but on this regime Penny has achieved so much. Her mother once told her to do one creative thing a day. 'That's what drives me, and sometimes I feel absurdly driven.'

Spending time at home raising three children meant this farmer's wife developed into a serious gardener. Among gardening peers she became known as the queen of vistas. The most striking of these is of Mt Tekoa in the Southern Alps, beckoning across a sloping lawn and ponds crossed by a slender arched bridge. They used a bulldozer to clear out overgrown shelterbelts and widen a stream to create this seemingly natural effect, and Penny planted trees that change with the seasons either side of a wide green lawn. But every room in the house has a view,

Previous page: Dawn on a still and calm deep midwinter's day at Flaxmere, with the rising sun lighting the flanks of Mt Tekoa. Before Penny came here all this was paddocks.
Top: Looking up the pond in spring with waterlilies emerging from the frozen water.
Bottom: In the rose garden Penny fattens the mix with foxgloves and peonies among many perennials.

and once you're in the garden your attention is adroitly drawn to the next intriguing area. Standing in the rose garden, you raise your eyes to a swathe of grasses and perennials, which in turn leads to green open spaces . . .

Her gardening efforts have helped carry the farm through the tough times, too. When the bottom dropped out of sheep farming in the 1980s, Penny dug up a paddock and grew gypsophila for the flower market, in the days when a bunch of gyp sold for $12 and a lamb fetched $6. She transformed the woolshed into a flower barn and employed locals to help pick, then dry and preserve the crop. And, on a roll, she established a nursery specialising in climbers and old-fashioned roses that she propagated herself. To show people what they were getting, she created a rose garden. She spent two years building a wall of rock unearthed from the paddocks and Penny is proud that the 130m of stone walls she has built over the years have all survived the predations of earthquakes.

Penny was a pioneer in garden tourism in the 1980s, though she says it happened by accident. After another dry year with no snow the local ski club was struggling, so she and John and friends opened their gardens as a fundraiser. It was such a hit they started a business called Country Gardens, and for the next 10 years they attracted tours and conference groups to the region. They had a ball, meeting people from all over the world. 'We brought people into our lives. The husbands enjoyed it and we all did cooking lessons.'

When John died suddenly in 1994, Penny's world changed forever. Everything went haywire, she says. Son Mark and siblings Sarah and Sam were just starting out on

Top: The tupelo *Nyssa sylvatica*, which revels in swampy conditions, is vibrant and colourful in autumn.
Bottom: In winter a clay pot matches its pale tones with frozen grasses and dying foliage.

their careers off the farm, and Penny decided to make a fresh start, too. She brought in a manager to run the farm and two partners to run the nursery, and she moved to Rotorua. But after three years there, ill health drove her home. It took four years to recover her strength, but Penny found solace in her garden. 'Getting your hands in soil is very therapeutic.'

Projects helped too — among them, transforming the tennis court into a marquee lawn, which was so successful that Sarah decided to hold her wedding reception there; it's now in demand as a wedding venue. In 2004 Penny started Art in the Garden with her friend Ali Meyer offering her property as a venue for artists to display and sell their wares and to help raise money for charity. Grooming the garden so it comes to life against a spring backdrop of azaleas and rhododendrons is a mission . . . and fingers crossed that the weather and the farm animals behave. The annual four-day event, which raises about $10,000 a year for two charities, has since been sold, but it's still held at Flaxmere. The new owner rents the garden from Penny — which, from her point of view, is so much easier.

Penny has achieved all this in a hostile, windy environment, at latitude 43° south and 330m above sea level, where temperatures range from -15°C to 40°C, not to forget years of drought and long, snowbound winters. Plants and people must be tough to thrive. You learn to be philosophical, Penny says.

She's also learned which plants will survive — mixing natives with exotics, favouring those that can cope with the altitude, rather than trying to be a purist. Always learning by doing and observing, Penny has travelled

Top: Penny's New Perennial garden inspired by her visit to Piet Oudolf, the Dutch master of this gardening style.
Bottom: What to do with smashed up gum trees after a storm? Turn debris into delight: the Whirlpool garden, with its central 'pool' of native sedge *Carex comans*.

extensively and seen plenty of gardens overseas. 'Every great garden has had an impact, particularly Ninfa in Italy with its very deep spirituality.' She's visited the garden of Dutch designer and plantsman Piet Oudolf, who opened her eyes to playing with colour in the landscape and merging it into the farmland beyond. Back home she decided to interpret his New Perennial prairie style using locally appropriate grasses and perennials. It becomes a palette of summer flowers among the softness of floating seedheads, 'truly wonderful,' she says.

Fifty years to the day since she began the garden, Penny embarked on a new project: a self-published garden memoir called *Flaxmere Garden: 50 years of extremes*. For her family, it's a moving legacy. 'I've always had to do things to attract people to the garden,' she says. 'It has to stand on its own feet financially.' What she's also tried to do, she says, is to blend the garden into the land beyond, to protect her view of Mt Tekoa from the house, and to revel in the changes that each season brings — which is why she calls Flaxmere a garden for all seasons and why it's recognised as a five-star garden of national significance.

Not long ago, when wind and snow damage proved too much for some of her shelterbelt trees, she bit the bullet and felled pines, poplars and gums to create a new garden area. She marked out a large circle with fallen gum tree branches and filled it with the New Zealand native grass *Carex comans*. This surreal whirlpool is an exciting centrepiece, the meeting point of one area of natives and another of exotics — and a splendid example of Penny making the best of what life brings.

Robyn Kilty
CHRISTCHURCH

IT'S DEEP, MISERABLE MIDWINTER, with rain pelting the deserted grey-washed streets. But here in a narrow innercity neighbourhood known for its Victorian workers' cottages, not all of which survived the earthquakes, a flash of colour makes you pull up. In front of a lively blue house with an orange front door, a towering clump of *Verbena bonariensis* has colonised a gap in the pavement. At this time of the year the purple vervain should be past its best, yet here it is, still with something left to give. Much too interesting even now to cut back, says its owner, artist and landscape designer Robyn Kilty. And if the garden behind it looks this good now, you can bet, come summer, it's a must-see.

Robyn has learned, through setbacks that would discourage less hardy perennials, to cherish plucky survivors. When she bought this old (circa 1870) cottage in the historic Englefield neighbourhood of Christchurch in 1993, it needed a complete overhaul. Patience and elbow grease transformed the workaday dwelling into a cute and liveable home — and its bare grounds into a popular destination for garden lovers. Number 11, as it's called, became a garden of national significance, a picture-perfect cottage garden that thrilled people nostalgic for pretty flowers all in a row.

Robyn's efforts extended beyond her picket fence: she got stuck into a project to enhance the local community. She helped form Friends of Beverley Park Heritage Rose Garden, and they, along with the local residents' association and the city council, pitched in to fashion a garden that Robyn had designed: heritage roses for a historic district, 150 specimens of 40 different varieties. Then came a season of earthquakes, starting in 2010, that left her homeless and her garden a ruin.

Clockwise from top: Flanking the orange front door a pair of lancewoods (*Pseudopanax crassifolius*) towers over Robyn's mosaic cartwheel 'welcome mat'; a slice of New Perennial planting featuring gazania, red orach (*Atriplex hortensis* var *rubra*) geum and euphorbia; the verandah is a favourite place to sit in the morning.

She found a haven with close friend Penny Zino (see page 232) at Flaxmere, Penny's large rural property northwest of the city, and it was their shared love of gardening that eventually perked Robyn up. In 2014 they had an extraordinary experience, she says. The women went to the Netherlands on a tour led by English designer and writer Noel Kingsbury to meet Piet Oudolf, the Dutch champion of an informal, naturalistic approach to gardening. The New Perennial movement favours ornamental grasses and perennials planted in swathes and encouraged to naturalise, in place of lawns and borders. They did a workshop at his garden. 'There's nothing more beautiful than grasses in the wind,' says Robyn.

Plus it's so easy to maintain: no mowing or pruning or weeding, as in traditional formal gardens. No more autumn clean-up 'to appease my tidy mind'. She lets her garden die down in winter then waits for plants to spring back to life as the season turns. She's learned to like a bit of messiness, she says.

And, as she quickly realised, this kind of planting would suit the prairie-like Canterbury Plains with its hot dry summers and snowy winters just as well as it suited her tiny city garden. 'It should all be adaptable to wherever you live and to your climate.' Choosing the right grasses is vital. Some overseas favourites such as Mexican feathergrass, *Stipa tenuissima*, are too invasive here. *Stipa gigantea*, on the other hand, is the summer focus in her front garden and she often recommends it to clients — it's not invasive because it doesn't set seed. *Anemanthele lessoniana*, *Deschampsia cespitosa* and the carexes can also give the look but not the headaches. 'I do like structure and a few New Zealand natives. And some naturalistic

Top: Robyn designed this elegant garden seat and painted it to suit its floral setting. White *Wisteria floribunda* 'Snow Showers' covers the pergola. **Bottom:** You can almost smell the fragrance of the 'Ghislaine de Feligonde' rose climbing around the old apricot tree. **Previous page:** *Verbena bonariensis* towers above Robyn's rejuvenated cottage in the historic Englefield quarter of Christchurch city.

gardens in Europe still have roses and hedges, so you don't get that died-back look.'

Before the quakes, the front garden at Number 11 had a traditional cottage look. 'I was getting sick of it and I was going to change it anyway. But people loved the box balls and roses, roses, roses . . . I had an arbour at the gate with climbing roses.'

Nowadays it's the same — but different — cottage garden, thanks to her Piet Oudolf tweaks. Old china lives on in colourful mosaic paths and paving, designed and laid by Robyn. And the planting scheme, which once favoured bright red and green, glows with oranges and purples and scarlet reds, growing through tufts of *Carex buchananii* and bronze fennel, nicely offsetting the cottage's grey-blue weatherboards. The quake-wrecked picket fence has been replaced by a wonkier version using demolition wood reclaimed from piles of rubble: Robyn wanted a jagged fence to symbolise survival. 'It looked awful when we first did it, but the colour ties it all together.'

Around the side and at the back all is bright and lush. Colours here are cooler, with a silver santolina hedge bordering beds of pink, blue and burgundy flowers, presided over by a glowing flamingo-pink garden seat that she also designed. Back here you'd never know now that the chimney had smashed to the ground, wrecking the house inside, or that her studio was a study in chaos and her vegetable patch a wreck.

Regeneration is something gardeners know about instinctively, but few of us have such a harrowing tale to tell. Robyn's garden is open to visitors again, now that the Garden City is slowly reinventing itself.

Top row from left: *Fritillaria imperialis*; the non-invasive *Stipa gigantea*; delphinium. **Middle row from left:** The stripy foliage of canna leaves; close-up of an Oriental poppy; the orange 'Temple's Favourite' tulip. **Bottom row from left:** 'Burgundy Iceberg' rose; *Geum chiloense* 'Mrs Bradshaw'; Tuscan kale *Cavolo nero*. **Above:** 'Burgandy Iceberg' rose in the vege plot, with santolina lined brick path leading to the garden shed.

Bev McConnell
WHITFORD

BEV McCONNELL SAYS SHE'S ONE of the luckiest people in the world. Turning 87 this year, she still spends time in her garden each day armed with secateurs and a keenly critical eye. Downing tools as usual at smoko time, she delights in the camaraderie and banter around the morning-tea table while work schedules are fine tuned. Her long-time lieutenant, the English-trained landscape gardener Oliver Briers, who has retired five times, may be there catching up with the very capable head gardener Ben Conway and the three younger members of the team — and an intern, perhaps, or a stellar garden expert visiting from overseas, or one of her horticultural friends who just happens to be passing. She may not have the strength to do a 12-hour shift with the barrow anymore, but Bev is still the hub of the universe she created half a century ago — a garden called Ayrlies that is world-famous in New Zealand.

When she talks about luck, Bev means here she is, still fully alive at her age, able to enjoy her garden. She has never taken for granted how fortunate she was in marrying Malcolm, who happily paid the bills for this ambitious venture of hers. In 1964 when they moved their five children out of the city for a new life in the country, she resolved to link their 48ha dairy farm to the coast below with a garden.

And she arrived with plans already nutted out, to fence off 1.2ha of paddock for a garden around the homestead and plant 500 trees for shelter. Gradually she expanded her reach, edging closer to the sea. Planting a native area below was the next link in the chain stretching Ayrlies from garden gate to coast. In the 1980s she bought 4000 liquidambar saplings to dwell in the valleys. The dream was finally realised in the new millennium when 14ha of wetlands

Top: Imagine you're a ewe leading your flock of sheep . . . that's the way Bev designed her natural-looking paths, to follow the contours of the land.
Bottom: A rowdy 'Scarlett O'Hara' bougainvillea brightens this green corner near the house come December.
Overleaf: The wetlands area is now a lure for birds and people, but creating a dam to contain the lake took decades of Bev's coaxing and planting and a massive engineering exercise. Such serenity was hard won and, for Bev, a dream come true.

were transformed into a habitat for wildlife. The final project is Bev's tribute to Malcolm, who died before he could see it finished.

Now, despite shortness of breath and the odd creaking joint, she has no plans to hang up her tools. 'I'm not fretting about it. If you are in the world you've got to keep going. I don't want to be in a chair dribbling.' Sensibly, though, she is planning for the garden's future. A long time ago she wrote letters to each of her children letting them off the hook: 'I didn't want them to be burdened with my dream.' They all wrote back saying it was more than just a garden, Ayrlies was their heritage and they wanted it to stay in the family. Despite its popularity with thousands of visitors each year, Bev says gate takings pay for only one staffer — in other words, the family pays most of the bills — and while 'we're very lucky to be able to do that,' other income streams are being explored.

Bev also wants to ensure the garden lives on in the way she sees it, as a large country garden featuring a seamless flow of informal borders, with detailed use of plant textures and colour, set against large lawns, ponds and waterfalls. With the future in mind, she's worked out a statement of intent: Ayrlies is a quintessential New Zealand garden of great artistry that nurtures the soul. Her vision: it's a spiritually uplifting garden treasure that inspires, heals and allows people to dream, an oasis from the ever-encroaching city.

She's also come up with a set of guidelines for managing the garden, when she's not at smoko to pass on the word. These are detailed and revealing; as well as advising on best-practice plant husbandry, they're also an insight into her artistic approach. So, plant in drifts, not spotted like acne. Have a plant at peak every week. Paths should follow the

Top row from left: *Passiflora quadrangularis* is a passionfruit with square stems and dainty skirted flowers; *Thunbergia coccinea,* a tropical vine from India; the Australian fuchsia *Correa backhouseana*.
Middle row from left: The hybrid hawthorn *Crataegus* x *grignonensis*; palm-fringed swimming pool by the house; *Rhododendron tuba,* a vireya from Papua New Guinea.
Bottom row from left: Curious bromeliad *Aechmea pineliana* var. *minuta*; a hot orange orchid, *Epidendrum radicans*; the American sweet gum *Liquidambar styraciflua*.

contour of the land, as though formed by an old ewe leading her flock.

Knowing how the magic is conjured does not undo the spell she's cast. It's always a treat when you walk through Ayrlies, ambling from one area to the next, breathing in clouds of scent, past beds that change gear from bright to pastel, never being hurried by intrusive signs. Plantaholics revel in the amazing diversity — better than in many botanic gardens, some say. Bev is an artist, which may explain why many are captivated by her painterly touch with colour, and the way she composes flower beds as if they're living canvases.

The benign maritime climate enables rather than dictates, encouraging fast tree growth and satisfying the demands of an international assortment of plant life, ranging from roses, succulents, tropical climbers and trees from North America to Norfolk Island, to native tree ferns. The sound of running water cascading down to the ponds has all been cleverly contrived by Malcolm's engineering skill and Oliver's design panache and hard landscaping, yet it feels as if these water features have always been there. Bev says she allows each garden area to have its own distinguishing feature, but their individuality should not be jarring — she wants the whole garden to be harmonious. Bev has chronicled the garden's ups and downs in a book, *Ayrlies: My story, my garden,* dedicated to her family.

Her efforts have not gone unnoticed. In 1998 she was made an Associate of Honour of the Royal New Zealand Institute of Horticulture (AHRIH), and she has been vice-patron of the institute since 2010. Ayrlies was one of the first gardens to open

Clockwise from top left: Bev's artistic touch with plant and colour combinations is evident here where silvery foliage (fat and feathery) and pink orchids snuggle up to deep red *Alcantarea imperialis*; to create such a naturalistic 'Niagara' falls which feeds and aerates the Cypress Pond was a major engineering feat for Bev's lieutenant Oliver Briers in the 1970s; one man and a digger built this waterfall too.

its gates to visitors through the RNZIH New Zealand Gardens Trust, and it's now a six-star garden of international significance. In the Queen's Birthday Honours list of 2010, Bev was awarded the Queen's Service Medal for services to New Zealand horticulture. In 2012 she was presented with the prestigious Veitch Memorial Medal, the only medal given outside Britain by the Royal Horticultural Society. And in 2015 she became a Member of the New Zealand Order of Merit (MNZM).

If you believe in magic, and trust that it can rub off, you could buy a plant from the Ayrlies nursery. Plant it in your garden — but heed Bev's favourite words of advice from Rudyard Kipling: 'gardens are not made by singing "Oh how beautiful," and sitting in the shade'.

Penny Wiggins
WARKWORTH

AT THE END OF A SUMMER not long ago, Penny Wiggins was bushed. Over 1000 visitors had been through the garden, a massive vote of approval from fans who come by the coachload to revel in this small slice of English garden gorgeousness. 'I don't know why,' she says. Could it be the sheer prettiness of the 0.8ha plot she and her partner Rowan wrestled from farm subdivision to a garden of national significance within 10 years — speedy by anyone's standards? Or her cheerful, infectious enthusiasm for sharing tips and tricks with fellow gardeners? Or the buzz you feel while you walk around among this cottage garden florabundance? If ever you were feeling blue, a visit to The Paddocks would be a rainbow remedy for what ails your spirit.

Penny is forever grateful to her mentor Bev McConnell (see page 252), who took her on as a part-time amateur weeder at Ayrlies, one of our best-known gardens, then gave her a fulltime job, nurturing her budding talent. 'It was the best day of my life,' says Penny. Apart from the day she and fellow Ayrlies gardener Rowan tied the knot.

So, when you garden for a living, what's your retirement plan — especially when your workplace for 15 years has been a class act? Start a new one, of course. They were looking for a small acre or two around Whitford (near Ayrlies) but could only find plots of 10 acres or more. Searching north of Auckland, they liked the feel of the (then) small country town of Warkworth and found just the thing: a newly subdivided farm on the outskirts.

Faced with a blank agricultural canvas, they cleared away farm equipment and a hawthorn hedge to create the house site. Earthworks yielded precious fertile topsoil that was put aside for raised vege beds in the yet-to-be-built

Top: The vege garden was the first area Penny started on. **Bottom:** The olive grove, which keeps family and friends in estate-grown oil, is the site of Penny's new shed. **Overleaf:** The view from the sheltered dining terrace, showing the lie of the land, from flower crammed border and potager, up the slope to the olive grove.

potager. Farmland soil already topdressed and bore-irrigated made for a running start — though nothing ever comes free. They were unaware of the area's high rainfall, but in a way it's a blessing, Penny says. Another surprise was severe frosts, which meant tailoring a plant list to suit. The worst pests were rabbits, but her always hungry Labradors couldn't be more delighted about that.

First on the list of projects came the potager, which needed to have easy access to the kitchen. Then the courtyard garden, where they could dine in privacy. 'We knew what we wanted to grow here and once I had planted my favourite David Austin roses and perennials, we moved on to the orchard.' Trees were progressively planted along the boundaries and from the driveway up to the house, joining all the dots.

From then to now: in 10 years the grassy paddocks have filled up with pretty and productive garden areas and plenty of favourite trees. The hillside above the house is an olive grove, bristling with 'Leccino' and 'Pendolino' varieties that keep the extended family in oil. The driveway with its trees is a calm green entry to the riot of colour beyond.

English-born Penny learned to love gardening as a tot from her green-fingered father and his head gardener, a man called Joyce, both of whom coached her efforts in her own little plot. No wonder she loves a dreamy English cottage-style of planting.

Around the house, the garden is a cleverly matched display of colour whose tonal range is gentle and subtle. There's a flourishing sea of fragrant, old-style roses — about 200 at last count — though Penny says if she had the room she'd have all David Austin's roses. She chooses roses that are old-school

Clockwise from top left: Foxglove spires poke up from shrub roses all chosen for their various subtle colours; pale terracotta is the perfect shade for the big pot in this central position; the lichen-encrusted gate was made from reclaimed tōtara; the apricot tones of old-fashioned climbing rose 'Crépuscule' warms the stone surface of this water feature.

and scented instead of modern and fussy. Favourites include her namesake 'Penelope', 'Winchester Cathedral', 'William Shakespeare 2000', 'Charles Austin' and 'Jean Ducher'. The climbers 'Crépuscule' and 'Souvenir de Mme Léonie Viennot' are happy sprawling over sunny fences, jostling for headroom in the background. Perky foxgloves make delightful, tall exclamation points among euro-sized pillows of flowers — foxgloves, unlike delphiniums, seem immune to slugs and snails here.

In her downtime from weeding every day (it's a real passion) and showing visitors around (she enjoys the company and the feedback), Penny likes nothing more than creating more plants. Daylilies, salvias and abutilons in hard-to-find colours emerge from her potting shed each spring to prettify another spot in her garden, or to sell. Other favourites to catch the eye are the pink and red dappled foliage of *Persicaria microcephala* 'Red Dragon', and the common but prettily scented herb valerian, which gains distinction in this company. In summer, look for verbascums, achilleas and salvias, with sedums and dahlias coming along a little later.

The vegetable garden, surrounded by a hedge of 'Beatson's Brown' coprosma, looks almost too good to eat, its decorative appeal underpinned by good gardening practice. Penny has always been a keen cook and caterer, so the sunny, well-composted plot is usually groaning with choice, and family, neighbours and charities are frequent beneficiaries of her abundant harvests.

Visitors will ask her what is the magic potion for her rumbustious rhubarb. The answer? Donkey 'do'. Elsewhere, Nitrophoska Blue. At the front, low teucrium hedges keep the

Top row from left: 'Charles Austin' rose; *Lysimachia atropurpurea*; 'H.F. Young' clematis.
Middle row from left: Babiana bulbs; Penny's garden journal; rose pink abutilon.
Bottom row from left: 'Abraham Darby' rose; Penny's secateurs are always by her side; *Tulbaghia fragrans*.

massed plants contained and disciplined — a good-housekeeping tip for busy gardeners, says Penny. *Teucrium fruticans* clips well into topiary shapes too.

Penny is an expert gardener who's happy to share her garden and her knowledge. 'Just keep plugging away at the weeding,' she advises. 'There's always something that needs doing, rather than leaving it to big bursts when you don't know where to start.' Catching one weed will save a million more, she says.

Her most useful tool is the notebook she keeps, a detailed diary of planting successes and setbacks — including plant names, which can prove elusive even for experienced gardeners when put on the spot. Workmanlike, sure, but like everything else Penny touches, it's beautiful.

Rosa Davison
MARLBOROUGH

IF ANYONE YOU KNOW HAS a serious case of native plant nausea, an affliction caused by exposure to dull municipal or motorway landscaping, the doctor is in. But the patient will have to drive down long back country roads to reach the place of healing at Paripuma, on the Marlborough coast south of Blenheim, where Rosa Davison has concocted the cure.

This talented landscape designer has created a beautiful native garden by the sea. It's a gardener's and cinematographer's dream: lush and green and open in equal measure, home to the rare and interesting as well as to ordinary everyday native plants. And, used with panache and given room to breathe, they all shine. Rosa's native garden is an instant pick-me-up.

Rosa likes to treat arriving visitors to a touch of drama. Hop off the coach or untangle yourself from the car and step into the enclosed courtyard between two wings of her stylish country house, where you'll be greeted with a cup of tea and a slice of homemade shortbread. You may notice a rustic wooden door, festooned with a pair of glossy emerald-green *Tecomanthe speciosa* vines. Shapely ngaio trees at the entrance face a pair of pots bearing Marlborough rock daisies. Neither tree nor daisy is rare, but here is where they belong and so they flourish. These are Rosa's scene setters, her statement of intent.

Tea finished, she throws open the door to the house and you look through the windows. That's when you clock a glimpse of a garden unfurling like a green carpet, its view across the sea to Mt Rahotia tugging you out to the terrace. It's a gesture that can leave people gasping with delight or, occasionally, bursting into tears. The discomfort of your journey is

Top: A judiciously tamed pair of *Tecomanthe speciosa* frames the charmingly rustic door in the entrance courtyard.
Bottom: Step through the doors to the terrace where Rosa's love for native plants is immediately apparent.
Overleaf: The garden unfurls towards Cloudy Bay with the ancient whale pot centred exactly on the peak of Mt Rahotia.

dispelled with the reward of a glorious garden framed by coast and cliff (pari means 'bluff' and pūmā, 'off-white' in Māori). 'I love the idea of giving people a bit of a shock,' Rosa says.

Wide steps entice you down into the park-like garden, with its curious centrepiece of a rusting ancient whale pot (a family treasure) and fire-bright Poor Knights lilies, *Xeronema callistemon*. From here on, Rosa lets people discover the garden at their own pace.

It helps, though, if you know that Rosa planted everything you see: when she and Michael and their three teenaged children moved here in 1999, this was all exposed sandy paddocks. Ask her how much land there is, and she jokes, 'depending on the tide, 5 or 7ha'. She remembers standing with arms outstretched, thinking, 'I want this to look as if we've cleared a space from the bush.' You be the judge.

Rosa drew plans for house and garden together, plotting it all down to the last detail, including the theatrical entry. Though she loved European formal gardens she never felt she should copy them at Paripuma — the bright antipodean light does exotic plants few favours. 'And how can you beat an English herbaceous border? They're fabulous, but I thought it would be fun to do a New Zealand version.' Rosa had grown up in the area and holidayed in the Marlborough Sounds as a child, so she knew which plants were sturdy enough to withstand the harsh coastal climate. She's not saying use only local plants: 'I love all plants. But why not use ours to better advantage?'

Rosa began at the borders, chipping through rock-strewn ground to plant windbreak gums (the 'ghosts of Gondwanaland', she calls them) and 2000 ngaio seedlings that

Clockwise from left: Looking up the coast to the dramatic white cliffs that gave Paripuma its name; a rare moment of peace in the duck pond; close-up of the massed display of Poor Knights lily *Xeronema callistemon*, their red flowers suggesting flames under the pot once used to render whale blubber.

she protected from wind-rock, possums and rabbits with haybales. As they found their feet, she followed up with generous quantities of ake ake (*Dodonaea viscosa*), *Coprosma acerosa* 'Hawera' for groundcover, hedges of hebes and *Coprosma repens* 'Middlemore', griselinia, puka, pittosporum and the buxus native alternative, *Melicytus obovatus*.

Rarities include a yellow flowered pōhutukawa, descendant of a pair found on Motiti Island in the Bay of Plenty. *Tecomanthe speciosa*, the elegant small tree *Elingamita johnsonii*, the aforementioned *Xeronema callistemon*, and one of the world's rarest plants, *Pennantia baylisiana*, were all rescued just this side of extinction from islands off the Northland coast and given a new home in Marlborough.

Rosa takes a laissez-faire approach when random seedlings appear. Mostly they're native plants such as ngaio, or weeds, and if they thrive that's fine by her. But she also propagates her own plants from seed, including lemonwood and tecomanthe, plus kākābeak (*Clianthus*) and the linen flax *Linum monogynum*.

When you reach the end of the 300m avenue, where garden melts into rocky beach, don't be surprised to find silverbeet, the commonest plant in Kiwi kitchen gardens, growing happily in the tide: it's floated up the coast, and Rosa lets it be.

Grass paths take you off the main divide through a tranquil nīkau grove that is one of her favourite areas. Elsewhere there's a handsome potager where vegetables grow in raised beds edged with railway sleepers; a scaled-down children's garden; and a native perennial area that is still under construction. Her next project is to merge the whole garden

Clockwise from top left: In the nikau grove; the curving trunk of a ngaio frames the access to a native perennial border garden down towards the beach; an elegant tool shed in the vege garden, the only area dominated by non-native plants; limbed-up ngaio *Myoporum laetum* line a path leading back to the main part of the garden.

OVERLEAF

Top row from left: Ngaio in flower; red flower of the Poor Knights lily; the shy flower of the Three Kings climber *Tecomanthe speciosa*.

Middle row from left: *Pennantia baylisiana*, once the world's most endangered plant; the native sea spurge *Euphorbia glauca*; the smallest fuchsia in the world, the creeping *Fuchsia procumbens*.

Bottom row from left: The small alpine shrub *Parahebe catarractae* 'Avalanche'; the orange-red flowering pōhutukawa *Metrosideros excelsa* 'Vibrance'; *Acaena caesiiglauca* is a native evergreen groundcover.

with the beach using plants that live on the saltwater margins.

One of Rosa's off-piste garden areas holds special memories: at Christmas it's red and glowing, thanks to a double row of the upright hybrid pōhutukawa 'Vibrance' flanking a red-painted bench seat. Rosa planned this when her mother, who loved pōhutukawa, was dying.

Rosa likes not being influenced by any designers or schools of thought: she doesn't want to do what everyone else has done. But if she's pushed to cite visual cues, she mentions the illustrated books she read as a child, with idealised landscapes that are still fresh in her artist's mind. 'I have a distinct memory of the clearing with the foal's grave in a Hans Christian Andersen book,' she says wistfully. She loves the freedom that formal design gives a gardener: get your clean straight lines right (and she admits she's fussy about this), fill it up to overflowing and it always looks tidy.

Nature has offered its own seal of approval with the return of tūī, kererū and korimako, quail, pheasants and grey ducks. The latter are descendants of a rescued duck, coddled in Rosa's bedroom until it was well enough to be released; three years in a row she has returned to raise her own brood. Rosa knows it's the same duck because 'she comes to my whistle and all the other ducks fly away'. This duck's growing family makes a beeline for the pond, home to hundreds of croaking frogs in summer ('the Kermit chorus'), plus geckos, insects and butterflies. Rosa is thrilled: 'It's given me the greatest pleasure of all.' She is a bit nuts about animals, she says. In fact, rabbits gambol unmolested here. After all, once seedlings are established, Bugs Bunny and co seem to lose their appetite for tougher older plants, she reasons.

Top: Rosa welcomes all creatures, even rabbits. This mature ngaio that's survived predators and coastal storms is now a living art work, thanks to Rosa's talent with a pruning saw.
Bottom: Looking up to the cliffs behind the house from the shrubbery near the duck pond. Hard to believe this was all just pasture a few years ago.
Previous page: A lateral view of the garden, looking up the avenue of pōhutukawa across to the pounding waves, a constant presence.

Rosa is modest about her achievements and genuinely delighted when people compliment her skills, or say this five-star garden of national significance has changed their minds about native plants. When she is praised for her floriferous display of xeronema, she demurs. There's nothing tricky about growing the famously difficult Poor Knights lilies here, she insists. Her prescription: plant them in rock, don't feed or water them, let them breathe in the wind, and chuck seaweed at them every now and then. It's easy.

Open garden details

Auckland district:
Omaio (Matakana)
Liz Morrow
www.omaio.co.nz

The Paddocks (Warkworth)
Penny Wiggins
rowan.penny@xtra.co.nz

Ayrlies (Whitford)
Bev McConnell
www.ayrlies.co.nz

South Taranaki:
Puketarata
Jennifer Horner
www.puketaratagarden.co.nz

Marlborough:
Barewood
Carolyn Ferraby
www.barewoodgarden.co.nz

Paripuma
Rosa Davison
www.paripuma.com

Canterbury:
Flaxmere Garden (North Canterbury)
Penny Zino
www.flaxmeregarden.co.nz

Number 11 Historic Cottage and Garden
(Christchurch city)
Robyn Kilty
www.robynkiltygardens.co.nz

The Giant's House (Akaroa)
Josie Martin
www.thegiantshouse.co.nz

Fishermans Bay (Banks Peninsula)
Jill Simpson
www.fishermansbay.nz

Dunedin:
Larnach Castle & Garden (Otago Peninsula)
Margaret Barker
www.larnachcastle.co.nz

Arrowtown:
Blair Garden
Janet Blair
john.blair@blairarchitects.co.nz

Acknowledgements

We are so lucky to have met such talented women. Can you imagine how daunting it must be when you're asked to show off your best beloved patch? It's demanding work primping a garden to a camera-ready standard, even for full-time gardeners, and when scribe and photographer come calling, the intensity of the exchange must be exhausting. For your dedicated work, generosity, courtesy, patience and good humour: thank you all.

Many went the extra mile on our two-year road trip, dispensing hospitality, knowledgeable advice and garden referrals, including Rick and Nina Acland, Margaret Barker, Fiona Farrell and Doug Hood, Jenny Glue, Elizabeth Goodall, Jane Kominik, Rose and Matthew Montgomery, Jan Morgans, Liz Morrow, Anne Noble and John Gray, Margo and Tom Pryde, Jill and Richard Simpson, Penny Zino.

Back home in Christchurch, Ken McAnergney smoothed domestic travails for wife Juliet, cooking gourmet meals often based on seafood he caught at Stewart Island. In Auckland Barb's husband Joe Macky, already a handy baker, became chief cook and bottle washer too, dispensing elegant cocktails when jittery nerves needed soothing. Our children were a huge support. Kudos and love, kids: Josie Nicholas-McAnergney, and the Macky clan, Oliver, Vanessa, Jasmine and Edward.

About the authors

Juliet Nicholas has been a freelance photographer for 30 years. Her work features regularly in New Zealand's leading magazines and this is her sixth book. An avid gardener, it's no surprise that Juliet is best known for her garden photography. When she is not taking pictures of other people's gardens, Juliet can be found pottering in her own Christchurch backyard, making up for bouts of neglect due to heavy work demands. In her downtime she escapes to the wilderness of Stewart Island, where she delights in the bounty and beauty of the great outdoors.

From newshound to book author, via tutoring, editing magazines both newsprint and glossy, and writing or editing several skiploads of stories, it's only taken Barb Rogers a few decades to work out what she wants to do — concentrate on writing about gardens and gardeners. A frustrated part-time gardener with one foot in Auckland city and one in the country, she longs for the patience and serenity that beckon from total immersion in one place. Meanwhile the weeds mount as she chronicles other people's green-fingered accomplishments and smelling their roses instead. This is her second book.

GODWIT

UK | USA | Canada | Ireland | Australia
India | New Zealand | South Africa | China

Godwit is an imprint of the Penguin Random House group of companies, whose addresses can be found at global.penguinrandomhouse.com.

Penguin
Random House
New Zealand

First published by Penguin Random House New Zealand, 2018

10 9 8 7 6 5 4 3 2

Text © Barb Rogers, 2018
Photography © Juliet Nicholas, 2018

The moral right of the authors has been asserted.

All rights reserved. Without limiting the rights under copyright reserved above, no part of this publication may be reproduced, stored in or introduced into a retrieval system, or transmitted, in any form or by any means (electronic, mechanical, photocopying, recording or otherwise), without the prior written permission of both the copyright owner and the above publisher of this book.

Cover and text design by Cat Taylor
© Penguin Random House New Zealand
Prepress by Image Centre Group
Printed and bound in China by RR Donnelley

A catalogue record for this book is available from the National Library of New Zealand.

ISBN 978-0-14-377090-9

penguin.co.nz